Power and Influence for Lawyers: How to Use it for Business Development and to Advance Your Career

Susan Letterman White, J.D., M.S.

WEST®

A Thomson Reuters business

For Customer Assistance Call 1-800-328-4880

Mat #41173653

ISBN 978-0-314-60273-2

Dedication

For Rachel and John;

And, in memory of my parents, Beatrice and Edward Letterman

About the Author

Susan Letterman White, J.D., M.S.

Susan Letterman White trains lawyers to think and act like business leaders through coaching, retreats, workshops, presentations, and other programs designed for a law firm, law department, or lawyer's unique needs including Crossing-Selling Strategy Teams for Business Development, Women's and Diversity Initiatives, and Strategic Communication for Career Advancement and Business Development. Outcomes of Susan's work include better and more productive business meetings, alignment and cohesion among an organization's lawyers, identification of strategic opportunities, conflict management, better team performance, and improved business performance. She was a practicing attorney in the area of employment litigation and counseling with more than 20 years of experience and a managing partner of a Philadelphia law firm before she began her Master of Science studies in Organization Development. She was awarded her Master of Science degree from America University with Academic Distinction for Exemplary Field Work. She is currently a faculty member in the AU MSOD Field Work course. Susan's background, which includes a J.D. from Loyola Law School and a B.A. in Philosophy from Brandeis University informs her approach to solving the problems that lawyers face. She is certified to administer and interpret the Myers Briggs Type Indicator® and experienced in administering and using the Law Practices Inventory® for leadership development and in the Thomas Killman Inventory® for conflict management training. She also has been trained in the use of organization network analysis, which she uses for uses to help her clients visualize the organizational structures and relationships that drive organization performance, employee engagement, and business development.

Additional information and a list of recent presentations, publications, and white papers is available on the Letterman White Consulting website at www.LettermanWhite.com. Also, visit www.LawyersLeadersTeams.com to see a list of programs and workshops. She can be reached at 610.331.2539 or SusanLettermanWhite@gmail.com.

Introduction

Power is energy and influence is a strategy. The purpose of this book is to help every reader become more comfortable and effective using power and influence to create a successful and happy life, however the reader defines success and happiness for herself or himself. I wrote this to help lawyers who have followed the best advice about how to achieve success and discovered that it hasn't worked as well as they had hoped it would. That advice—to work hard, do a good job, and success will follow—turns out to be grossly inadequate for most of us. This book is intended to help readers put aside an outdated way of thinking about success and try something new—a research-based strategy to achieve one's goals and personal vision of success.

I practiced law for over 20 years, became the managing partner of a law firm in Philadelphia, and switched careers to become a consultant for law firms and a coach for lawyers before the idea of this book ever crept into my mind. I have felt powerful in a courtroom, deposition, and over a meal when talking about my work. I have also felt powerless when I unsuccessfully tried to convince my partners to embrace the idea of a transformational change to our business model and when I twice tried to get on the preferred provider list of two separate clients' insurers. In sharing my experiences, I discovered that many lawyers have also experienced similar feelings of frustration when using power and influence strategies outside of their professional role as lawyers. These shared experiences led me to wonder: Why are lawyers extremely powerful and influential when acting in our professional capacity but often uncomfortable and feeling powerless when trying to advocate for ourselves and develop new business, advance our careers to the highest levels, or lead our firms in a new direction? More importantly, I began to wonder: What can we do to differently to increase our chances of being successful in all aspects of our professional and personal lives? I wrote this book to answer these questions and help readers learn how to develop a comfort and skill set in using power and influence to create success for themselves.

To that end I have included three learning streams. First, there are stories and advice from in-house counsel in large organizations, partners in law firms, a small firm owner, a law school dean and professor, a federal court judge, and government lawyers. These are stories of lawyers who are happy with their careers and, in particular, the daily experiences of their jobs. These stories provide lessons by example that a reader might apply in addressing his or her challenges. The pieces of advice offer ideas to consider. Second, there are theories, models, and other explanations of the key concepts in this book. They key concepts are offered as a linear way of thinking about the factors that affect one's ability to influence outcomes. I define key concepts such as "Power Bases" (sources of energy) and "Influence Strategies" (a strategy is plan with a series of steps that is designed to attain a specific goal) and offer models and processes for identifying goals, approaching challenges, and designing processes to influence the decisions of other people. Models are helpful as checklists and visualization tools for developing and practicing new skills. Third, there are worksheets for taking the information from the first two learning streams and using it in practice to develop the deeper skills necessary to address the reader's personal challenges and reach his or her goals.

Power, Influence, and Other Important Terms Defined

Think of this book as an instruction manual for developing power and influence skills. The terms that will be used in this instruction manual need definitions. Simply put, power is energy and influence is a strategy to use power to reach a goal. A strategy is a plan that is designed to attain a specific goal. When the plan is detailed with a series of steps or actions that must happen for the strategy to succeed it is termed an Action Plan. When a person reflects on his or her actions and experiences and analyzes their origins and usefulness in attaining goals, this is called Action Learning, and it is based on intelligent experimentation with trial and error.

Power Bases are the personal sources or types of energy that vary from person to person. A person can expand an existing **Power Base** or develop a new one. This book explains five different **Power Bases**. An **Influencer** is a person who uses his or her specific **Power Bases** as part of a deliberate **Influence Strategy**, which is a strategy with a series of steps designed to affect the decision-making and behavior of a **Target** in ways that the **Influencer** thinks will bring about an intended outcome and move the **Influencer** closer to his or her goals.

The definition of an **Influencer** is related to the definition of leadership as an ability to affect others' beliefs, attitudes, and courses of action.[1] As such, this book is about leadership as much as it is about anything else. This book is not theoretical, although it includes theory. It is a practical handbook to use as a tool for advancing one's career and developing a substantial book of clients and business, which makes it useful for attorney development programs. It is also a useful tool for law firm or organization leaders, who are responsible for leading teams, groups, and meetings toward measurable goals and outcomes. However, advancing one's career and developing a book of business only matter if they are related to one's definition of success and the related personal goals. Leading teams and meetings only matters if they are related to the organization or group's purpose, vision, and goals.

The Power and Influence Process Model and Organization of This Book

This book is organized according to the five components of The Power and Influence Process Model: (1) Personal Goals and Definitions of Success; (2) Thinking about Power and Influence; (3) How Decisions are Made; (4) Personal **Power Bases**; and (5) **Influence Strategies**. This model will help you organize your experiences, thoughts, and skill development.

The first component of the model is one's personal goals and definitions of success. The desire to achieve goals and become successful creates a "felt-need"[2] for developing and expanding **Power Bases** and **Influence Strategies**. Like any effective strategy, **Influence Strategies** do not exist in a vacuum. On the contrary, they exist because of a person's broad objective and supporting goals, which emerge from his or her beliefs about what success means and what will bring happiness. Research tells us that effective strategies are energized and directed by a high degree of motivation to achieve a particular outcome or reach a particular goal.

Influence Strategies will be more or less effective because of the next three components of The Power and Influence Process Model: the ways in which an **Influencer** thinks about power and influence; the decision-making processes used by a **Target**; and the **Influencer's** personal **Power Bases.** How we think about

---

[1] Peter G. Northouse, Leadership 7 (4th Edition 2007).

[2] Joan V. Gallos, Organization Development 140 (2006).

anything influences the decisions we make and the actions we take. Our fears are obstacles and our motivations are catalysts. Our definitions, thoughts, and feelings about power and influence are lenses through which we see or lenses that obscure our view of critical information and opportunities. Unless we know how others make decisions, we cannot design an effective influence strategy. We need to know whom to influence and how that person or group is susceptible to being influenced. Finally, **Influence Strategies** depend upon leveraging our personal **Power Bases** in particular ways. To do that, we need to identify our **Power Bases**, be aware of what we are missing, and develop our opportunities to add or strengthen our personal **Power Bases**.

Each chapter of this book, except for the final one, begins with a description of the chapter's content and questions for the reader to keep in mind while reading the chapter. Each chapter ends with a summary of the key points. Diagrams are included to help the reader understand the concepts. Assessments are included to help the reader think about his or her skill level. Worksheets are for the reader to develop skills, collect data, or create an action plan. Personal stories of power, influence, and success are included to explain concepts and as case studies to learn what these concepts look like in the real world.

Why Are Some People Successful and Others Not?

Why are some people successful, powerful, and influential, while others appear not to be? Is the managing partner, who reluctantly serves in that position, personally successful? Why do some people quickly advance up the ladder in your organization while others stagnate or even languish? Why are some people great rainmakers and others not? Job performance and competence are only part of the story of success and not nearly as strong influencers of success as you might believe.

The link between some standard job performance metrics and career advancement is weak. Jeffrey Pfeffer puts it this way, "contrary to what most people think, they are not responsible for their own careers." In contrast to what many are taught to believe is true, "being politically savvy and seeking power are related to career success."[3] Research suggests that if the person who is in a position to evaluate your performance and advance your career also hired you, you will have a better chance of getting ahead; salaries are more closely correlated with the age and organizational tenure of the person than performance;[4] and educational credentials are more closely correlated with internal mobility than overtime work, absence, or job performance.[5] Finally, getting noticed, developing relationships with mentors, sponsors, and important decision-makers, and influencing how your accomplishments will be measured are much more important than actual performance.[6] In view of the relationship between some performance metrics and advancement, it becomes our responsibility for being noticed, remembered, and likeable by others. We can do this by acting in ways that leaves them "feel[ing] good about themselves."[7] Developing skills and strategies to get noticed and known by those influential and powerful others for what you do well and have accomplished and then influencing them to help you attain your goals is the purpose of this book.

---

[3] Jeffrey Pfeffer, Power 4, 20 (2010).

[4] Jeffrey Pfeffer, Power 23 (2010).

[5] Jeffrey Pfeffer, Power 24 (2010).

[6] Jeffrey Pfeffer, Power 25-26 (2010).

[7] Jeffrey Pfeffer, Power 35 (2010).

Table of Contents

CHAPTER 4. PERSONAL POWER BASES

CHAPTER 5. INFLUENCE STRATEGIES

Chapter 1

Personal Goals and Definitions of Success

KeyCite®: Cases and other legal materials listed in KeyCite Scope can be researched through the KeyCite service on Westlaw®. Use KeyCite to check citations for form, parallel references, prior and later history, and comprehensive citator information, including citations to other decisions and secondary materials.

---

§ 1:1   Chapter focus and questions

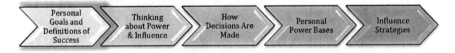

This chapter explains the relationship between defining success and happiness and identifying goals for oneself and developing the motivation to act in ways that will advance your career. The only reason that people *need* **Power Bases** and **Influence Strategies** is to achieve their goals. People are motivated to act in particular ways because of their particular goals. For purposes of motivating action, the most effective professional goals are those that are also connected to one's personal goals, values, passion, happiness, and definitions of success. Goals also inform an **Influencer** of the decisions that need to be made in his or her favor and the **Targets**, who will make those decisions.

This chapter also explains the importance of building sufficient motivation to expand and develop one's **Power Bases** and **Influence Strategies** and how to do that. Sufficient motivation to do the work, which will lead to expanding and developing one's **Power Bases** and **Influence Strategies**, is a consequence of the presence of three conditions. There must be a desire to change one's thinking and behavior, a clear vision of what the change means to the person, and an awareness of the first steps necessary to achieve the change. Together, these three conditions must be greater than any resistance the person feels toward making the change.[1]

Questions to consider as you are reading this chapter:

- What is success?
- What are your goals?
- How will your definitions of success affect your use of power and influence?
- How are your goals connected to your career advancement or business development strategies?
- How do you know whether the three conditions that must be present before you will be sufficiently motivated to expand and develop your **Power Bases** and **Influence Strategies** are present for you?

§ 1:2 Personal goals and definitions of success motivate one to act in ways to attain those goals and personal success

Goals are the steps taken toward creating a life that aligns with a person's vision of success and happiness. When an **Influencer's** vision of success is closely intertwined with his or her

---

[Section 1:1]

[1]Warner W. Burke, Organization Change, 141 (2008).

happiness, there seems to be an added boost of energy for that person to use in facing the inevitable challenges in life. The absence of a clear connection with one's happiness seems to produce inertia.

Dean JoAnne Epps, Dean of Temple University Beasley School of Law, attended Yale Law School and was a Deputy City Attorney for Los Angeles and an Assistant United States Attorney before joining the faculty at Temple in 1985. If she were starting out as a lawyer today, she would "give [herself] permission to be ambitious and set goals." She advises her students to "dream about the kind of life you would like and think about the best way to achieve it." Dreaming is the precursor to determining one's happiness, ideas of success, and vision for the future. Dreams lead to a vision, which leads to goals.

Laura is the division counsel to a health care company. She advises lawyers to "start with being aware of what you really like to do and look for a job that lets you do more of that." So much of a lawyer's time is spent in the office. "If you don't enjoy it on a day-to-day basis, it's hard to get the energy to do what you need to do to advance" your career and feel successful. Figuring out what makes any person happy is impossible without sufficient self-awareness of one's identity, in particular how to spend one's time to create deep enjoyment in life.

The responsibility for figuring out the circumstances that will bring deep enjoyment, creating a vision of the future, and choosing specific goals is a personal and nondelegable responsibility. Ritva Sotamaa has had a remarkable career to date. Currently, she is the General Counsel of Siemens AG—Healthcare Sector. She began her career in Helsinki, where her husband and children remained as the speed of her career trajectory escalated and took her to the Milwaukee, Wisconsin, the UK, and eventually Germany. Her advice to young lawyers is that ultimately everyone is responsible for his or her own career and happiness in life.

Setting personal goals plays a critical role in directing and maintaining behavior and is important in career decision-making.[1] Goals motivate. People face inertia every day and will change the way they think and act only when have a deep desire for some state of affairs that they believe will make them feel a

---

[Section 1:2]

[1]Bryan J. Dik, Adam M. Sargent and Michael F. Steger, Career Development Strivings: Assessing Goals and Motivation in Career Decision-Making and Planning, 35 Journal of Career Development 23 (2008).

specific emotion like happiness or a sense of success, whatever that means to them personally.

Wanting to attain a particular goal is an example of wanting something to be different.[2] Feelings of success, passion, hope, inspiration, and joy are particularly strong motivators and uniquely personal feelings and beliefs. Each drives significant and tangible accomplishments.[3] These feelings and beliefs will influence each person's choice of goals and actions to achieve those goals. "[W]hen individuals commit themselves to a goal, they are highly motivated to achieve it."[4] Further, the more motivators working together, the stronger the force in a particular direction.

Creating a conscious and unambiguous vision of your future, knowing with detail the circumstances that will bring you happiness in your life, and defining goals with specificity will increase the likelihood that you will develop the necessary skills and use them effectively to influence the future that you want. Each person's path to success is unique. The path to becoming a General Counsel of a large international organization is different from the path to owning a solo general practice firm. The paths to partnership in two different firms are different and there are also differences among the paths to partnership in the same firm because of the different starting places and identities of each lawyer.

None of this is to suggest that happiness, ideas of success, and goals are static. They change over time as a person has new experiences that broaden that person's perception of his or her world and thinking about that world. As they change, plans will change too. That's a topic addressed in more detail later in the book.

Worksheet: Creating Your Vision of Success Story

Choosing appropriate goals begins with identifying a personal vision of success. Try writing down a description of the different factors that together you believe will constitute a successful life.

---

[2]Brenda B. Jones and Michael Brazzel, The NTL Handbook of Organization Development and Change 29 (2006); John P. Kotter, The Heart of Change 15 (2002); Jane Magruder Watkins and Bernard J. Mohr, Appreciative Inquiry 38–39 (2001).

[3]Rosabeth Moss Kanter, Does Your Passion Match Your Aspiration? http://blogs.hbr.org/kanter/2010/03/does-your-passion-match-your-a.html?loomia_ow=t0:s0:a38:g4:r1:c0.000000:b0:z6 (last visited June 16, 2010).

[4]Edward E. Lawler III and Christoper G. Worley, Built to Change 241 (2006).

- To do this effectively, you need to know what you want and what will bring you happiness.
- This will probably depend on your passion, values, and principles.
- It will also depend on where you are in your life. For example, the reason that you wanted to become a lawyer before you entered law school might be very different from the reason that you want to remain a practicing lawyer today.
- It will also depend on how you think about success. Is it related to happiness? If so, how? What circumstances will help you to feel happy and successful?
- What specific goals, if attained, will create the circumstances that will help you to feel happy and successful?

The greater the detail in your vision of success, the easier it will be to stay on a path toward becoming successful. For example:

- Identify the circumstances that will be different and better if you become an equity partner in your law firm, double your business generation next year, become the General Counsel of your company, the dean of your law school, or attain any of your goals.
- Specify how you expect to feel as you move closer to your goals. These feelings will also serve as guidance to keep you on the right path toward your goals. Influencing intentional changes in the behavior of other people begins with being able to effectively influence yourself. In particular, you must want to change the way that you think about and use power and influence.

Goals motivate action and serve a second purpose. Certain goals may also serve to build up specific **Power Bases**. If you want to work for a particular law firm, in a particular industry, or for a specific organization, you may need to have had certain experiences first. For instance, if you want to work in politics, you may need to give yourself certain experiences and place yourself in specific networks before attaining your dream job in politics presents itself as an opportunity for you. If you want to clerk for a United States Supreme Court Justice, you may need to have specific experiences in law school, including a degree from one of a handful of law schools. It is important to clearly define for oneself what success means and the unique goals that are related.

Case Studies: The Importance of Goals

Carol (Carrie) Hogan is a partner and the head of the Product

5

Liability Practice at Jones Day. Carrie is national coordinating counsel for Laboratory Corporation of America's professional negligence litigation related to its Pap smear testing. She represents The Sherwin-Williams Company in its nationwide lead paint litigation brought by state attorneys general, local and state governmental entities, and private plaintiffs. She also has extensive experience managing and coordinating nationwide litigation programs for clients such as The Chamberlain Group, Experian Information Solutions, LabCorp, and TRW for the Chicago Office.[5] By any measure, Carrie is an extremely successful lawyer. She is also a happy lawyer. She attributes her success as a partner in a large international law firm to her goals.

Like most lawyers, Carrie describes herself as goal-driven. However, for Carrie, the personality trait of being goal-driven is only the tip of the iceberg. She believes that setting personal goals and keeping them present in her thoughts on a daily basis is responsible for her success:

> I think that lawyers are goal-oriented people. We do well in school so that we can get into a good law school. Then we strive for good grades in law school so that we can get a job at a good law firm. Then we want to make partner. We have goals for individual victories in trying cases. I'm always thinking about my goals. At some point, you have to set goals for yourself because the profession stops offering them. What's my goal now that I'm a partner? What am I doing now? I've set goals for myself, like being a good mentor, developing business, and being a good representative of my law firm. I have a deep sense of loyalty to my firm and I am always aware of that and trying to be a good face for Jones Day. I want to be a great trial lawyer and for my clients to feel like they are getting their money's worth. I want to be a great mentor. Everything that I do is defined by those goals. I'm about to get on a plane to see a client. I could send someone else, but I don't want to. I'm always thinking. "It's good to be needed." Nobody likes lawyers until they need one.

Let's look closer at Carrie's past and present goals:

- Getting good grades
- Getting into a good law school
- Getting a job at a good law firm
- Becoming a partner at her law firm
- Being a great mentor
- Developing business

---

[5]Jones Day Web site, http://www.jonesday.com/chogan/#0%3D0%261%3D %23ctl00__MiddleCenter__attorneyForMiddle__ctl00__tabProfile%262%3DProfi le%263%3D0%264%3D0%265%3D0%266%3D10%267%3D%268%3D%269%3Dtr ue%2610%3Dtrue%2611%3D%2612%3D%26 (last visited March 15, 2011).

- Being a good representative of her law firm
- Being a great trial lawyer
- Generating a feeling or conclusion in her clients' minds that they are getting their money's worth
- Feeling needed by her clients

First, her goals are action words and phrases about something she has done or will do. Implicit in her goals is the belief that she controls whether they are accomplished or not. She does not list a goal that depends on someone else's power and **Influence Strategies**. In other words, her goals are not that someone else does something and then she feels happy, although they may include a component of influencing someone else to do something.

Next, some of Carrie's goals are past goals, which have created a strong foundation of power for her to use in her **Influence Strategies** of the future. For instance, getting good grades, joining a good law firm, becoming an equity partner, and winning victories for her clients have helped her to build a strong professional reputation as a winning and powerful litigator in her field. Other of her goals can be thought of as destinations, which she aims to visit repeatedly and she acts in way that make the visits possible. She wants to obtain more victories for her clients, be a "good face" for her law firm, be a great mentor, develop more business, and be a great trial lawyer. Yet other goals represent feelings that she wants to generate for herself or her clients. She wants her clients to feel or believe that they are receiving good value from her services and she wants to feel needed by her clients. These emotional mindsets will motivate her to continue acting in ways that create more personal successes and motivate her clients to trust her and continue to choose her to represent them in the future. Carrie's goals serve multiple objectives.

Carrie has willingly gotten on an airplane to visit a client, despite a long day at work and the option of sending someone else. She wanted to be needed by her clients and believed that the action of getting on a plane after a long day's work to visit a client would engender that feeling in the client. Carrie's choice to fly out to meet her client was clear because she was motivated by multiple goals. In addition to wanting to be needed by her clients, she also wants her clients to feel as though they are getting their money's worth and to be a "good face" for her law firm. Multiple goals are seem to have a synergistic effect in motivating behavior.

Ronne Kaplan's ideas of success and goals were very different from Carrie's. Ronne was driven by a passion for politics. She attended law school with the idea of being involved in politics to make the world a better place. When she was in college she worked on the campaign of Gene McCarthy, who was running on an anti-Vietnam War platform,[6] a cause she fervently supported. It was on McCarthy's campaign that she met Arnie Miller. Miller asked her to work on Jimmy Carter's campaign and when Carter won, Kaplan received a presidential appointment, which eventually led to her role as Special Assistant to the Deputy Assistant Secretary of Education, an ideal job and connected to her goals at the time.

There is evidence that having a clear idea of success and setting goals is a very effective factor in bringing about one's career success. Interestingly, many of the people that I interviewed for this book attained a high level of success without setting clear goals for themselves. It is worth pondering whether these people would have attained even more success, or success at a faster pace, if they had set goals. Regardless, two related theories may be emerging. Many of these people were of the Boomer Generation, women, and lawyers of color. First, it's quite possible that this is a generational difference. For example, the youngest person interviewed, Nikki Johnson-Huston, was clear about having a vision and goals. She was also clear that she valued power as a tool for achieving her vision of being inspirational for others and changing the world for people who grew up like her. Nikki, an African American woman, grew up homeless and without an intact family. Second, some of the stories suggested a possible difficulty or reluctance in dreaming or envisioning the details of a successful future for oneself that is connected to the absence of role models and socioeconomic, gender, and racial privilege in one's life.

Dean Epps, when interviewed, said that if she were starting out as a lawyer today, she would "give [herself] permission to be ambitious and set goals." What stands out is the word "permission." Dean Epps is an African American woman, who grew up poor and with parents who were not professionals. She did not have access to the world of professionals until she was an adult. Her experiences of exclusion included "being on the fringes of a conversation" where a group was discussing whether they preferred London or Paris for a vacation and she had never been out of the United States.

It is quite possible, and beyond the scope of this book to investigate further, whether there is an additional hurdle to developing a vision and setting goals for people who lack certain privileges. In any event, given the research in support of envision-

---

[6]Wikipedia, http://en.wikipedia.org/wiki/Eugene_McCarthy (last visited March 4, 2010).

ing and goal-setting as motivating factors, it is worth facing the possible challenge inherent in the tasks, despite the possibility that one might be lucky enough to have opportunities for success emerge on their own. The better able you are to identity your goals, i.e., the things that you want in life, the easier it will be to ask for those things or take any other steps to make it more likely that you will realize them.

§ 1:3 Definitions of success and specific goals are necessary but not sufficient without the motivation to change one's thinking about developing and using Power Bases and Influence Strategies

Power Bases are the individual sources of different types of energy available to use in any **Influence Strategy** to attain one's goals. The more **Power Bases** available and the better designed and implemented the **Influence Strategies**, the more likely it is that one will attain one's goals. It is possible to have unambiguous ideas of happiness, success, and goals, and face challenging obstacles blocking one from doing the preparation work to expand one's skill set to expand and develop one's **Power Bases** and **Influence Strategies**. The motivation to change this type of thinking and behavior results from a burning desire to change the way one thinks about and uses **Power Bases** and **Influence Strategies** because of a clear understanding of how making these changes will make a positive difference in one's life and an awareness of the initial steps to take to precipitate the changes. These three factors must outweigh the level of natural resistance to making any change in one's thinking and behaviors. The burning desire is consequence of knowing what you want. This is your vision, sense of happiness, and specific goals. There is evidence of positive outcomes connected to power that may give you a clear understanding of how power is related to what you want. There is evidence of each of the following connections with the effective use of power. Career success is related to seeing power and being politically savvy. People with greater political skill received higher performance evaluations and were rated higher as leaders. People with power live a longer and healthier life. Power is related to status, wealth, and getting things done. Human beings are driven to seek power.[1] Awareness of the initial steps for precipitating these changes in thinking and behavior are developed by participating in workshops, peer leadership groups, and practicing the new ways of thinking and behaving.

[Section 1:3]

[1] Jeffrey Pfeffer, Power 4–8 (2010).

Finally, motivation grows when one addresses the natural resistance to making any change in one's thinking and behavior. Adults naturally resist making mistakes and the loss of psychologically important routines. Mistakes are inevitable when learning a new skill. It's hard to imagine learning to ski without ever stepping on one's skis. Every behavioral change involves thinking or doing less of something to open up the space to do more of something else. If you intend to exercise more, you inevitably must be less sedentary. The closer the mistakes and loss are to a person's core identity, the harder it becomes to change thinking and behavior.

Research suggests that motivation grows when a person develops an interest in acquiring new skills and improving knowledge despite making mistakes,[2] since mistakes are inevitable when learning new skills. This means that motivation grows as a person changes his or her attitude toward making mistakes. Lawyers, in particular, fear making mistakes. Professionally, it is malpractice. Lawyers think of mistakes as bad. In business, mistakes are data to use in revising a strategic plan. They are opportunities to learn and generate ideas of different actions to try to affect a better outcome.

Ritva Sotamaa has worked in many different cultures as her career advanced. "Often when you start in a country you go through a learning curve of how to cope in the particular culture. You adopt new ways of expressing yourself, such as levels of assertiveness, often through a fail and learn type of path." Without a willingness to try different ways of participating in discussions to find out which approach will be more or less effective in any situation, it is harder to learn what will be most effective and influential. Having the right attitude toward challenges "has a big role." Ritva describes herself as enjoying challenges, courageous, and someone who isn't easily frustrated.

Changing one's behavior is a transition and regardless of whether a person is eager or reluctant to change the way he or she thinks and acts, changing either will feel like a loss of familiar routines. As a loss, the resistance to making any change will increase with the psychological importance of the loss.[3] This means that motivation grows as a person acknowledges the loss and changes his or her attitude toward it. The more significant

---

[2]Antonio Valle, Ramon G Cabanach, Jose C Nunez, Julio Gonzalez-Pienda, et al. Multiple goals, motivation and academic learning, 73 British Journal of Educational Psychology 71, 72. Retrieved March 15, 2011, from ProQuest Education Journals (Document ID: 324982651) (2003).

[3]W. Warner Burke, Organization Change 91 (2008).

the loss, the more important and challenging it will be to change one's attitude toward it.

One of the most familiar and psychologically important routines of lawyers is the dependency on and use of argument or logical persuasion as an **Influence Strategy**. It is part of a lawyer's training and for many lawyers the training was merely polishing the thinking and skills that had been practiced since that person could speak. Superimposed on that training are years of practicing those particular skills with other lawyers, juries, judges, friends, and families. The routine use of verbal power in the form of logical argument is psychologically important to every lawyer. Indeed, more than one lawyer interviewed for this book defined power as "the ability to persuade," a term of art among lawyers. For some lawyers, this type of power and **Influence Strategy** is also a strong manifestation of their identities.

Persuasion, through the use of rhetoric, is only one way to influence people. In fact, despite a likely belief of many lawyers to the contrary, logic and reason is not the process people use to make choices. Using other **Power Bases** besides being an expert and other **Influence Strategies** besides logic and reason means using less of the pool of skills that is closely intertwined with a lawyer's identity. Using less of this type of power and **Influence Strategy** will feel like a loss of a familiar routine to most lawyers.

Thus, it is highly likely that most lawyers will be resistant to changing their thinking and behavior, despite understanding that they are adding more to their **Power Bases** and **Influence Strategies**. Although adding new ways of thinking, new **Power Bases**, and new **Influence Strategies**, these changes will feel like a loss.

People experience a strong aversion to loss and become more attached to what they perceive they control and less aware of what they may gain. The "aversion to loss is a strong emotion."[4] Lawyers will perceive a loss of a familiar routine by using a prized form of influence less; all people perceive changing how they think as a transition. "Every transition begins with an ending. We have to let go of the old thing before we can pick up the new one," and this phenomenon superimposes an additional feeling of loss in "definitions of who we are" as lawyers and individuals.[5] The best way to counteract the resistance to change created because of the perception of significant losses is to build motivation to make the change by focusing on the expected gain. In this

---

[4]Dan Ariely, Predictably Irrational 134 (2009).
[5]William Bridges, Transitions 11 (2004).

case, it is an increase in the available options to use in any **Influence Strategy** to achieve any career goals.

Following are tools to help you assess your resistance and develop your personal motivation to start the transition in how you think about using power and influence.

Worksheet: Measuring Your Motivation and Resistance

For each question, mark the box that most closely corresponds to your reactions to each statement.

1. I do not believe that there are any problems associated with my use of **Power Bases** and **Influence Strategies** to address challenges and obstacles in my life.

Strongly Agree	Agree	Neutral	Disagree	Strongly Disagree

2. I do not think any changes in my **Power Bases** or use of **Influence Strategies** are necessary.

Strongly Agree	Agree	Neutral	Disagree	Strongly Disagree

3. I think there are a few problems associated with my use of **Power Bases** and **Influence Strategies** to address challenges in my life, but no changes are needed.

Strongly Agree	Agree	Neutral	Disagree	Strongly Disagree

4. The only changes around my use of **Power Bases** and **Influence Strategies** to address challenges in my life have been a result of pressure from others.

Strongly Agree	Agree	Neutral	Disagree	Strongly Disagree

5. The way that I use **Power Bases** and **Influence Strategies** to address challenges in my life is at times effective and at other times ineffective.

Strongly Agree	Agree	Neutral	Disagree	Strongly Disagree

6. I would like to improve the way I use **Power Bases** and **Influence Strategies** to address challenges in my life, but I am skeptical about my options to make a difference.

Strongly Agree	Agree	Neutral	Disagree	Strongly Disagree

7. I would like to improve the way I use **Power Bases** and **Influence Strategies** to address challenges in my life, but I am skeptical about my ability to make a difference.

Strongly Agree	Agree	Neutral	Disagree	Strongly Disagree

8. I would like to improve the way I use **Power Bases** and **Influence Strategies** to address challenges in my life, but I see significant benefits to keeping the status quo and difficulties in trying to change it.

Strongly Agree	Agree	Neutral	Disagree	Strongly Disagree

9. I would like to improve the way I use **Power Bases** and **Influence Strategies** to address challenges in my life, but I am not sure about my ability to sustain a change.

Strongly Agree	Agree	Neutral	Disagree	Strongly Disagree

10. I would like to improve the way I use **Power Bases** and **Influence Strategies** to address challenges in my life and see the positive and negative aspects of this. I know that if I become more effective in the way that I use **Power Bases** and **Influence Strategies** that the benefits will outweigh the costs of making the change.

Strongly Agree	Agree	Neutral	Disagree	Strongly Disagree

11. I am committed to developing and expanding my **Power Bases** and **Influence Strategies** and willing to do whatever is necessary to that end.

Strongly Agree	Agree	Neutral	Disagree	Strongly Disagree

12. I have begun to develop and expand my **Power Bases** and **Influence Strategies** and have noticed a difference in my effectiveness in reaching goals.

Strongly Agree	Agree	Neutral	Disagree	Strongly Disagree

Instructions for Interpreting the Worksheet and Diagnosing your Level of Motivation

Agreement or strong agreement with the first two questions suggests that you are not motivated to change the way you think about and use **Power Bases** and **Influence Strategies**. You first must reflect on how you are thinking and then consider alternate ways of thinking. Your motivation to learn the techniques and develop these skills is weak. Agreement or strong agreement with questions 3 and 4 suggests that you are beginning to reflect on how you are thinking about **Power Bases** and **Influence Strategies** and to consider changing the way you think. Your motivation to learn the techniques and develop these skills is beginning to grow. Agreement or strong agreement with questions 5–9 suggests that you are reflecting on how you are thinking about **Power Bases** and **Influence Strategies** and considering how to change your thinking and behavior to make a positive difference. Agreement or strong agreement with questions 10 and 11 suggests that you are strongly motivated to build your **Power Bases** and **Influence Strategy** skills. Agreement or strong agreement with question 12 suggests that you have begun to experiment with new ways of expanding and using **Power Bases** and **Influence Strategies**.

Worksheet: Building Motivation to Develop and Expand Power Bases and Influence Strategy Skills

Motivation is the set of driving forces that determine a

behavior. Resistance is the set of restraining forces that inhibit a behavior. Skill development thrives on the motivation to successfully develop the skill. Expanding or developing one's **Power Bases** and **Influence Strategies** is a skill and requires one or more changes in behavior. The driving and restraining forces for changing behavior fall into the following categories: Desire, Ability, Reasons, and Commitment. Desire refers to one's wants, hopes, and dreams about what might become possible after the new behavior is in place. Ability refers to the physical, intellectual, and emotional skills necessary to make the behavioral change. Reasons are the logical arguments in favor of making the change. Commitment is the dedication to changing the behavior.

For each category, develop a list of the Driving Forces and Restraining Forces. Building a list of driving forces that outweighs your restraining forces will increase your motivation.

	DRIVING FORCES	RESTRAINING FORCES
Desires		
Ability		
Reasons		
Commitment		

Worksheet: Developing Motivation by Envisioning the Future

To develop motivation, ask the following questions:

15

- How will circumstances improve if I start acting intentionally to make a difference in my life?
- What is so important to me in life, personally and professionally?
- What is my vision for my future professional life?
- What are my guiding values and principles?

Worksheet: Developing Your Personal Goals and Definitions of Success

People are influenced by the stories they tell themselves. In as much detail as possible, write the story of what success for you will look and feel like as a result of developing and using **Power Bases** and **Influence Strategies** effectively. To help you write this story, answer the questions below.

1. What are your values and principles? What is so important to you in life, personally and professionally?

_____

_____

_____

_____

2. What are the responsibilities and benefits of advancing within your organization?

_____

_____

_____

_____

3. If applicable, what are the privileges of controlling a significant book or business?

_____

_____

_____

_____

4. What do you want? What does a successful future look like for you?

_____

_____

_____

_____

5. What are your personal and professional goals that depend on your effective use of power and influence?

_____

_____

_____

_____

6. Describe your current professional situation in terms of where you are, what you have achieved, and your current challenges. _____

_____

_____

7. Draw the journey map that shows your pathway and major events that have taken you to where you are today professionally.

8. Draw the journey map that shows your pathway and major events that will take you into the successful future that you envision for yourself.

§ 1:4 Chapter summary

- Personal visions of success and identification of goals serve as motivation to face challenges and choose the actions that will help develop business and advance your career. They also serve as information to guide the choices of who to target in an **Influence Strategy**.

- Building sufficient motivation to do the work necessary to expand and develop one's **Power Bases** and **Influence Strategies** will help a person navigate through the natural resistance to making any changes in thinking and behaving. Sufficient motivation arises from wanting to change one's thinking about and use of **Power Bases** and **Influence Strategies**, believing that making such changes is connected to achieving one's personal vision of success and goals, knowing how to make the changes, and facing the natural resistance to making mistakes and feeling a loss of a familiar and important routine.

Chapter 2

Thinking About Power and Influence

KeyCite®: Cases and other legal materials listed in KeyCite Scope can be researched through the KeyCite service on Westlaw®. Use KeyCite to check citations for form, parallel references, prior and later history, and comprehensive citator information, including citations to other decisions and secondary materials.

---

§ 2:1   Chapter focus and questions

Personal Goals and Definitions of Success → Thinking about Power & Influence → How Decisions Are Made → Personal Power Bases → Influence Strategies

This chapter explains how one's hidden beliefs and feelings, both about what constitutes a challenge and the appropriate ways to address challenges, affect one's actions and chances of attaining his or her goals and visions of success. It is easy for an **Influencer** to inadvertently become an obstacle to his or her ability to design and implement an effective **Influence Strategy**. This is because the way a person thinks about power and influence will have a direct effect on that person's ability to notice his or her **Power Bases** or cultivate additional ones, design effective **Influence Strategies**, and use his or her **Power Bases** effectively in **Influence Strategies**. The way a person thinks about power and influence will serve to push that person forward or hold that person back.

This may sound easy, yet for most people, the way they think is like an invisible, odorless, and tasteless ether that affects the decisions they make and the actions they take. This process of a person's thought patterns affecting his or her actions happens out of one's conscious awareness and certainly without one's consent. The last chapter explained how a person's definitions of personal success and goals affect his or her thoughts and actions, including the motivation to expand and develop one's **Power Bases** and **Influence Strategies**. This chapter can be summed up this way: When in the role of an **Influencer** facing a challenge, make sure to get out of your own way!

Questions:

- What thoughts and feelings do you associate with the words, power, influence, challenge, and conflict?
- How does the way you think and feel about challenges and conflict affect how you use your **Power Bases** and implement your **Influence Strategies**?
- How can you change your thinking and feeling about challenges and conflict?
- What are your default responses to challenges and conflict?
- What other ways can you respond to challenges and conflict?

§ 2:2   Changing the way you think about using power to address your challenges—Dr. Carol Pearson and the Hero's Journey

The way one thinks about challenges, i.e., how one defines them and what one considers to be reasonable responses, will affect what one notices and the decisions about appropriate responses. Dr. Carol Pearson, in the 1980s, developed a model to explain possible responses to challenging situations, which she called the Hero's Journey, named after Joseph Campbell's work,

The Hero with a Thousand Faces, a compilation of comparative mythology. Campbell theorized that the myths from around the world have prevailed over time because they share a common structure, which explains something fundamental about the human condition. Pearson's model consists of six archetypes: the Innocent, Orphan, Warrior, Wanderer, Martyr, and Magician. These archetypes are examples of different ways to use **Power Bases** and **Influence Strategies.**

One's choice of a **Power Base** or **Influence Strategy** is often a consequence of how that person thinks and feels about a particular challenge. A challenge occurs when a person experiences conflicting wants, needs, or expectations or an obstacle on the pathway to a particular goal or vision of success. A conflict in wants, needs, or expectations may take the form of internally driven inertia to a change in thinking or behaving or an obstacle in the form of a missing skill. Alternatively, it may be an external obstacle, such as the conflicting wants, needs, or expectations of another person. The resistance that people experience to making any change in their thinking and behavior is also a challenge. The perception of a challenge or conflict triggers the need to use **Power Bases** and **Influence Strategies** to move past the challenge or conflict and closer to a particular goal.

One's emotional responses to challenges affect one's choice of actions. For some people, conflict "arouses strong feelings [that] interfere with [his or her] ability to think strategically"[1] and notice the opportunities in educating a person on a different perspective, finding out why someone thinks differently and collaborating to leverage differences and innovate. "Because more people are conflict-averse they avoid . . . paying the emotional price of standing up for themselves" in a productive way.[2] This includes lawyers acting on their own behalf. A person who is reluctant to ask for what she or he wants, like a work assignment, a mentor, a promotion, or raise, is less likely to get it. Without appropriate data about what you want, a person who has the power to influence the decision to give you what you want won't know that there is a need to exercise that power. Jane Dalton is a recently retired partner from and presently of counsel with Duane Morris LLC. She advises, "do not be afraid of success or failure. Fear of failure can be paralyzing; fear of success will limit the opportunities you see for yourself."

[Section 2:2]

[1]Jeffrey Pfeffer, Power 169 (2010).

[2]Jeffrey Pfeffer, Power 53 (2010).

One's response to a challenge depends on his or her thinking, feelings, skill level, and the particular challenge. Learning how to identify the thoughts that lead to the use of a default reaction to challenges opens up the possibility of relying on more than one's default reactions. Identifying the thoughts behind actions is the bailiwick of cognitive behavior theory.

Cognitive behavior theory first looks at perceptions, what a person notices in his or her world. The theory then explains that the way a person thinks about a perception affects how that person feels about that perception and, ultimately, what that person will do as a result of how he or she thinks and feels. An external event "elicits a thought." The thought might be an "evaluative judgment." The thought then "elicits an emotional response." If a person changes the way that he or she thinks about that perception, that person can change his or her feelings.[3] However, this change process can be very difficult when it requires the person to change his or her deeply held beliefs. These beliefs are "based on attitudes or assumptions from previous experiences."[4] Beliefs, sometimes termed stories, mental models, paradigms, or schemas, are the lenses through which people notice and interpret data. They affect a person's ability to see or ignore information and to interpret it.

People tell themselves stories about the limits of their **Power Bases** and **Influence Strategies**. These stories affect their beliefs about what they can do and then their actions about what they will do to respond to a challenge, such as asking to lead a key initiative within their organizations. The stories that people tell themselves about what they can do to achieve success are developed and influenced by the stories that are part of our society. These stories are the framework of news accounts, fictional literature, movies, mythology, advice, and criticism. As historian Francis M. Cornford once said, "[t]he mind of any individual . . . is not an insulated compartment, but more like a pool in one continuous medium—the circumambient atmosphere of his place and time."[5]

A person, who wants to advance his or her career, develop a significant client base, or become a leader within his or her organization must identify the stories that will affect their responses to challenges and change them if necessary. Thus, one needs a

---

[3]David Rock and Linda J. Page, Ph.D. Coaching with the Brain in Mind. 300–01 (2009).

[4]Morley Segal, Points of Influence 151 (1997).

[5]Francis M. Cornford, Thudycidides Mythhistoricus viii (1907).

way to identify their stories. Studying Pearson's archetypes is a useful tool for identifying the various ways in which people respond to challenges and one's very personal and often hidden stories.

§ 2:3 Changing the way you think about using power to address your challenges—The Innocent

The Innocent archetype does not notice challenges or conflict, is trusting, and depends on others for direction. This may be because the Innocent's context is an idyllic paradise, he or she is inexperienced, he or she is oblivious to the challenges and dangers that are actually present, or because the Innocent is intentionally focused and ignoring distractions. At some point, the Innocent realizes the presence of challenges and/or conflict. Maybe this happened on your first day in law school, in your first job after law school, when the economy changed, or your first time in court.

Dara Green is a former airline pilot and fifth-year associate in the tax department at the Miami, Florida office of Baker & McKenzie, LLP. Dara, who focuses her practice on foreign tax planning, is also 51 years old. The pathway to her position wasn't easy. It was a transformational change. She was a successful airline pilot for a major U.S. carrier, when, in her 40s, she learned that she would be losing her job in a matter of months. This is an example of an Innocent's paradise transforming into a place of challenges.

Every archetype has a vulnerability and a power. The vulnerability of the Innocent is in not noticing serious risks and wonderful opportunities. The power of the Innocent is in the ability to ignore the insignificant distractions on the pathway to one's goals.

Consider the example of Carrie Hogan getting on an airplane to visit her client after a very long, hard day of work. What if she had focused her thoughts and energy on her health? Perhaps her sense of exhaustion would have taken on more prominence. What if she considered that she would be giving up an evening at home and the benefit to her personal life by doing that? What if she thought too much about her other, equally important clients and their needs? There is tremendous power in being able to remain focused on a singular goal at any moment in time. The Innocent's power to ignore distractions is incredibly powerful.

Worksheet: Diagnosing Your Innocent Thinking

Answer the following questions to assess your Innocent tendencies:

1. Are you missing out on opportunities?
2. Are you late in noticing risks?
3. Are you constantly distracted from what you need to do to attain your goals by too many opportunities, risks, or ideas?
4. Do you believe that all you need to do to be successful is to be a good lawyer?

Interpreting Your Responses

If you answered yes to questions 1, 2, and 4, you are probably telling yourself stories about your power and influence that are biased toward Innocent tendencies and the result is that you are not as well prepared as you could be to seize opportunities or effectively manage the risks that are actually present. Advancing your career and developing business demand that you seek out and notice opportunities. If you are not noticing what you need to do, who can help you to do it, and where those opportunities are, you run the risk of remaining stuck in a position or thinking that there are not business development opportunities.

If you answered yes to question 3, you are probably telling yourself stories about the importance of extreme vigilance. This may also be a consequence of a personality trait of being easily distracted. Remember, there are times when it is ideal to rely on your Innocent tendencies, including those instances when extreme focus on a particular task is necessary. The key is being able to identify those times and choosing the Innocent stance.

§ 2:4 Changing the way you think about using power to address your challenges—The Orphan

Orphans are extremely adept at noticing and identifying dangers and protecting themselves and others through **Influence Strategies** that rely on their expert abilities. They see the world as a place that is full of problems and themselves as the bearer of the solutions. They do not rely on anyone other than themselves because they don't believe they can count on anyone else. They see themselves as the experts who are alone capable of eliminating the dangers. If you are thinking that this sounds a lot like what lawyers do for their clients, you are right. This archetype fits with the classic, expert-dependent relationship and power dynamic. Lawyers value this type of power, especially when it is paired with an **Influence Strategy** based on logic and reason. Indeed, this is the skill that every lawyer needs to have to be effective in the practice of law. This power is somewhat ineffective for addressing the challenges that require deep relationships, innovative solutions, and collaboration.

More of Dara's story. She had not finished her undergraduate degree at the time she lost her job as an airline pilot. Once she made her decision to become a lawyer, she completed an additional 48 credits for her undergraduate degree and major, finished law school and an LLM program in Taxation, and landed an associate position in the elite law firm of Baker & McKenzie in four years.

Dara's loss, in her 40s, of a profession that she loved and which was her identity created a challenging journey that she approached in a way that transformed her. The way she explains it is this:

> I did what I had to do. What else could I do? What can an airline pilot do when you're 44 years old and lose your job? I'm not a superwoman. I had no choices. I had to start all over and make a living. I never saw that I had that many options. [Law] was the only job without [going to medical school] where I could get my income back.

She acknowledges the high price she paid, "I lost my husband in the deal," because once hired by Baker, she was in the office and working long hours five or more days a week and the adjustment to the new career took its toll on the relationship. Dara Green took an Orphan's approach to her situation and solved her problem counting only on herself to face her challenge and she was rewarded with incredible success.

There are times when the Orphan archetype might not be an effective strategy to employ in advancing a person closer to his or her goals and definitions of success. If you are the General Counsel and Corporate Secretary of a Fortune 50 company and the CEO tells you that she wants to take a particular action that will significantly advance the company's goals, but all you see are every obstacle to taking that particular action, you may be giving accurate legal advice, which will protect the company from a significant risk, but you aren't collaborating like a strategy partner. One perspective on the situation is to notice a risk and figure out a way to avoid the risk. A better way of thinking about the situation might be to find the opportunities to move the company closer to its strategic goals in the face of risks. A better action might be to listen closer to what the CEO really needs, wants, and expects and then to help the CEO find a solution that will enable her or him to help the company to reach its goals while managing and monitoring any risks.

Typical Orphan business development behaviors for lawyers are attempts to persuade a client to hire the lawyer because of his or her expertise as a lawyer. Orphans expect to be hired for jobs or advance their careers because of their skill level and performance alone. Sometimes this works; often it does not. Diane Elderkin is an outstanding patent litigator. Her jury awards and professional accolades tell the story. Diane will tell you that although she continues the marketing technique of cold calling potential clients who have been sued if she thinks her team would be an ideal fit, it has yet to lead her to landing a new client. Most of the time, most people won't be influenced to choose a particular lawyer because that lawyer is the best lawyer for the job. Her tenacity may pay off one day, especially if she is able to add a second strategy to the mix. For instance, if the trusted advisor of a potential client that she cold calls, tells the potential client that Diane's team is ideal for the job, it might improve the outcome.

How much of the Orphan's tendencies do you incorporate into your approach to challenges and conflict? Orphans tend to distrust others and believe that expertise rests in individuals who are separate from the problem. In the expert dependency model one party is the all-powerful, in-control expert, who will solve the problems of a fully dependent other. When the Orphan cannot solve a particular problem, he or she finds another expert. Does this sound like the lawyer-client and lawyer-expert witness relationships that you know? This perspective isn't as helpful in solving the problems that require innovative solutions and collaboration or those that arise when working in government, a team, leading others, developing deep client relationships, or in-house.

The Orphan's tendency is always to see danger and decide to single-handedly fight it. Orphans think of themselves as facing challenges alone and solely responsible to protect themselves or others from any danger. Some situations call for this behavior. Other situations may not. Everyone has a default preference in responding to certain challenges. Consider whether the Orphan preference is one of your strong default preferences.

Worksheet: Diagnosing Your Orphan Thinking

Answer the following questions to assess your Orphan tendencies:

1. Do you tend to blame others for their behavior and not consider how changing yours could make a difference?
2. Do you blame yourself for not solving problems that are actually outside of your control?
3. Do you tend to believe that problems are created and solved by others and your job is to stay out of the way?
4. Do you tend to believe that you can solve any problem if you just put your mind to it?

5. Have you frequently changed coaches, mentors, or jobs in search of a better situation and find yourself still unhappy with your career advancement or business development efforts?

6. Are you avoiding getting a coach or mentor or finding a new job because you believe they will not make a difference in improving your career prospects, performance, or goal attainment?

7. Is your trust of others set at a low or high default?

8. Do you often feel as if you have been or are at risk of being abandoned or exploited in your job?

9. Do you refuse to rely on others because you believe you will only be disappointed?

10. Are you extremely independent?

Interpreting Your Responses

If you answered yes to many of these questions, you are probably telling yourself stories about your power and influence that are biased toward Orphan tendencies and the result is that an Orphan-type response is your default action when you are facing a challenge, including those associated with advancing your career or developing business. Remember, there are times when it is ideal to rely on your Orphan tendencies. The key is being able to identify those times and choosing the Orphan stance rather than to have it kick in as a default reaction to any challenge.

§ 2:5 Changing the way you think about using power to address your challenges—The Warrior

Warriors look at a challenge and see a struggle against somebody or something. They think the solution will emerge along with the victor. The Warrior's role is to vanquish an enemy. Where the Innocent might not have noticed a challenge and the Orphan might have interpreted a challenge as distinct from a person, the Warrior interprets a challenge as a conflict between parties. The parties may be individuals, a group, or an organization. The Warrior may represent himself, herself, or a third party. There are sides in the conflict perceived by the Warrior and the other side is the enemy.

This should sound like a familiar dynamic. Lawyers are taught the set of Warrior behaviors in law school, where the battle skills of advocacy are honed. In my work with lawyers and firms, I see more Orphan and Warrior behavior than any other. Warrior behaviors are very effective in the right situations; however, the right situation is not always present. It is important to recognize when the situation is not right for a Warrior stance, which is not always obvious or even fair.

When Reneé Bergmann was in her first year of law school in the midst of first semester finals, her grandmother passed away. The funeral was on a Sunday and she had an exam on Monday morning. She asked for a time adjustment and was denied. She was told that she could not have extra time, despite the obvious traumatic event, and that since the funeral was on Sunday, she was physically able to attend her final on Monday. She was told that in the real world you don't get an extra day if something bad happens:

> I did what I had to do to get to a Sunday funeral and return to my Monday final. Once I came to the understanding that this was just something I had to do, once I was told 'no,' I accepted that. I didn't continue to confront or fight it. I accepted it and moved on.

The Warrior's power is the courage, assertiveness, and confidence that is helpful in asserting for oneself, protecting others, enlisting allies, and getting up when knocked down in the metaphorical battle to advance one's career or build a book of business. There is an equal amount of courage and confidence in deciding against a Warrior stance as Reneé did.

Warriors lead their troops by giving clear direction about what to do, when to do it, and how to do it. They are very good at expressing their needs, wants, and expectations. They get what they want through the power of forcing, if necessary. They use the resources under their control to impose their will on others.

The vulnerability for individual Warriors is that relationships can be shattered as a result of a win-lose paradigm. The Warrior needs to win at the expense of someone else's loss. The additional vulnerability for groups of Warrior lawyers is stagnation, rather than movement toward a shared goal. In the extreme, a lawyer will expect and even attempt to force others to conform to his or her needs without any sense of what it means to be in relationship with colleagues or clients. In my consulting practice and in facilitating retreats and workshops, I frequently work with groups of lawyers that find themselves in violent agreement with each other. They debate ideas that are essentially the same instead of building on the shared ideas until a solution emerges. For the Warrior, a sense of identity comes from feeling different and stronger than "the other." When a Warrior begins to value relationships with others and understand responsibility to others, the Warrior learns how to use her or his strengths most effectively.

Dorian Denburg faces challenges using the best strengths of a Warrior and managing against its risks. Dorian is president of The National Association of Women Lawyers and General Attorney for AT&T. She helped AT&Ts predecessor avoid $600 million in expenses through her work on numerous federal and state cases of first-impression and first-of-its-kind legislation. Dorian created a national program to guide law firms in developing and solidifying relationships with in-house counsel. Dorian was the first outside counsel invited by AT&T's predecessor, Southern Bell, to come in house. Dorian had a champion, who helped open a door for her by creating a position for her in the Atlanta headquarters. She moved her family from Miami to Atlanta to take the position.

Like many women, Dorian thought that "work hard and you'll succeed" was a strategy for a fulfilling career. She now advises others that "knowing the rules" for advancing your career within any particular organization is critical. She thinks of power as "influence, opportunities and opening doors."

The way she approaches professional challenges is informed by the experiences in her personal life. She has three children. Her son was diagnosed with Autism shortly after the birth of her twins. Her daughter successfully battled Leukemia. About significant professional challenges, she says, as the mother of a special needs child and another who survived cancer, "if you have something tough to handle, I can handle it; I've handled tougher." She sees herself as a "very positive person. It is not enough to be a survivor. I am a thriver." She is oriented to challenges by her belief that although you do not have control over the hand you are dealt, "you have control over how you play your hand. I choose to play my hand and win."

Dorian is an extraordinary networker. She connects people with one another.

> I really enjoy connecting with people. I've never been anywhere in the world where I don't see somebody that I know. I enjoy learning about people and connecting people to each other. I find out about a person. Who they are is as important as what they do. The world is small and when you talk to people the world gets smaller.

Dorian is courageous, assertive, and confident when faced with any challenge. She also nurtures relationships and tries to help others by figuring out what people need, their goals, and their motivations. "I create deliverables, try to help people, and strive to win," she says.

It can feel great to be part of a Warrior's team if the Warrior leads by clearly articulating a vision that resonates with team members, designating complementary roles and responsibilities for each person on the team, and fairly rewarding the contributions from each team member. A government lawyer who directs approximately 75 employees and between 50 and 100 full-time consultants at any time does exactly that. She explains that she doesn't believe in rigid structures or job descriptions. Instead, most of her job descriptions "are porous" where "people are often doing things that are shared across unit lines." She explains her leadership strengths as being "very good at defining a strategy and pushing it out as far as possible" by "figure[ing] out what the skill set of each person is and tailoring job responsibilities to play to people's strengths." This design is extremely effective because she supports those people in "learning new things."

§ 2:6   Changing the way you think about using power to address your challenges—The Martyr

In contrast to the Warrior, the Martyr's sense of identity and strength flows from feeling connected to and deeply caring about someone or something other than oneself. As a developing leader recognizes his or her connection to others in the larger network of a team, practice group, division, organization, industry, and his or her world, she or he starts to see how his or her actions affect others. The Martyr does the proverbial right thing even when it means sacrificing his or her own interests, wants, needs, or expectations for the good of others. As with the other archetypes, at the extreme end it is a vulnerability. Certainly, this is what parents do for their children without thinking. The vulnerability results from a blurring of boundaries between oneself and others and prevails until a person learns how to manage those boundaries. This shows up when a person is unable to ask for what he or she wants, needs, expects, or deserves. It is present in someone who is rarely able to decline a request to help. The following example of the Martyr archetype is of a partner's decision to act in the interest of a larger group instead of the partner's personal goals.

The partners of Howry, LLP voted to dissolve on March 9, 2011; however, reports suggest that the demise started more than a year before that when key partners began to leave.[1] The exodus

---

[Section 2:6]

[1]David Latt Howrey LLP. RIP: Partnership Votes to Dissolve http://abovet helaw.com/2011/03/howrey-llp-rip/ (last visited March 19, 2011).

of key partner and groups often precedes a firm's demise.[2] One lawyer interviewed reported that a close friend, who was a partner at Howry, felt that the right thing to do was to stay until the end and remain aligned with a group which was negotiating to move to Winston & Strawn. Winston eventually rescinded all offers to Howry partners in Washington, D.C. That's an example of Martyr behavior.

Martyr behavior has a strength, too. Imagine being involved in an argument with someone, knowing that you are right, and avoiding the conflict because allowing the other person to win will position you for advancing your interests or ultimate goals. Effective win-win negotiation is another example of the strength of Martyr behavior on both sides.

A senior partner in a large law firm was less than a month away from reaching an age under which the current partnership agreement would have vested his right to receive a significant payout from his capital account if he chose to retire or otherwise leave the firm. For financial reasons, some members of the firm wanted to restructure the partners' capital accounts in a way that would significantly reduce the shares and value of capital accounts of many of the partners at the firm. This senior partner influenced other partners in the firm to agree to this reduction in their capital accounts and to raising the age at which the accounts would vest as a result of leading by example, because it was in the best interests of the firm itself to make this restructuring.

One lawyer interviewed advises attorneys who want to advance their careers that it is just as important to manage up as it is to manage down. The people who will make the decisions about your life, to whom you report, need a high degree of attention. Your goal should be to be highly responsive to them and make them look good. He says that you should be happy if they are taking credit for your work. They have power over your career and are more likely to think positively of you if you are responsive to them and make them look good. When someone you report to asks you to do something, you have to find the time to do it promptly regardless of whether you have other work that demands your attention and regardless of how important you perceive the request to be. That doesn't mean that you can ignore your other work, but it does mean that you have to find time for the work of the people who control your future, including work-

---

[2]Susan Letterman White. What Can We Learn from the Implosion of Wolf Block? http://www.law.com/jsp/pa/PubArticleFriendlyPA.jsp?id=1202430274626 (last visited April 29, 2009).

ing extra hours if necessary, regardless of how important you perceive that work to be. This advice highlights the importance of your relationships with those who have the power to make the decisions that affect your goals, especially your career success. It is one of the strengths behind the Martyr archetype.

Consider whether your default thinking about challenges aligns your behaviors with the Warrior or Martyr archetypes. Are you able to ask for business, a raise, or a promotion? Do you make sure that those who will evaluate your performance know what you have contributed? How do you talk about your successes and with whom?

Worksheet: Diagnosing Your Warrior and Martyr Thinking

Answer the following questions to assess your Warrior and Martyr tendencies:

1. Is your default mode of interaction or communication a confrontational process designed to produce a winner and a loser? (Too much Warrior)
2. Is your default mode of interaction or communication a process that avoids confrontation? (Too much Martyr)
3. Is your inclination to tell others what you want and need and then expect them to satisfy your needs and wants? (Too much Warrior)
4. Is it your inclination to ask others what they want and need and then make every effort to satisfy them regardless of the impact on your own wants and needs? (Too much Martyr)

§ 2:7   Changing the way you think about using power to address your challenges—The Wanderer

Wanderers use the combination power of autonomy and independence like a sword, rather than the shield it was in the Orphan stage. They are clear about their boundaries, unlike Martyrs. They have no desire or need to fight like Warriors. Wanderers will separate themselves from the confrontation dynamics that the Warrior find alluring and the rescuing dynamics that the Martyr finds alluring. Wanders respond to a challenge or conflict by changing their context. The context might be a particular employer, career choice, geographic location, division of a company, or anything else that defines a place and time for him or her. Wanderers are able to see the limits of their effective use of **Power Bases** and **Influence Strategies** and know whether those limits are because of obstacles beyond their control or undeveloped skills, and then make appropriate choices to create a better situation.

Where a Warrior would likely never give up, a Wanderer would notice that he or she cannot influence a person who doesn't feel a need or want for the something to be different. A Wanderer also notices whether he or she is able to satisfy the **Target's** wants, needs, and expectations. If you are in a context where your powers of influence are ineffective because those whom you need to influence are intractably resistant, then the best exercise of your power might be to change your context. This is the power to find a better organization or set of target clients. If the organization is not presenting a person with the right opportunities or denying opportunities altogether, a Wanderer will leave. A Warrior might sue. A Martyr might stay for the benefit of others in the Organization or his or her family.

Law firm lawyers who are Wanderers are often lawyers with high portables or a niche expertise that is highly coveted in the marketplace. Sometimes Wanderers are at a point in their careers where they want to try something new. Stephen Louis, Chief, Division of Legal Counsel of the New York City Law Department said that he advises young lawyers to try other jobs. He tells lawyers not to be afraid to move around because that's the only way to get a better sense of what you are really interested in and to get a different perspective on your career. It wasn't until Louis left city government for a job in a law firm that he realized he belonged in city government. Changing jobs, not simply changing offices, exposed him to an entirely new outlook, which was invaluable to him. In both his city law role and law firm role, he was responsible for advising the New York City governmental agencies on issues arising in transactions. He learned to appreciate the different interests, pressures, wants, needs, and expectations of each role. Having had the power to wander, Louis was able to learn what he really wanted for his career and collect additional information about the different pressures of each role, thereby making him a more effective and powerful lawyer when he returned to city government.

There are systems in which being a Wanderer is an effective way to gain experience and build relationships that are necessary to ascend to higher positions. This may mean changing organizations and is part of Steven Stein Cushman's "odd" pathway that he followed to his current position as Chief of the Contracts and Real Estate Division of the New York City Law Department. His first job with the City of New York was right out of law school. He started in litigation and left after five years to work in the City's Department of Environmental Protection. He then returned to the Law Department in the Environmental Law Division where he was part of the team that negotiated the New York City Watershed Agreement over a two-year period. As part of that effort, he drafted and negotiated 30 contracts. While doing that, he built relationships with the people in the Contracts and Real Estate Division. When a job in the Real Estate Division opened up, he was then asked to take it. In 2004, his division chief retired and he became the Chief.

The vulnerability of the Wanderer is that, in the extreme, they are lawyers who are never satisfied being part of any team, practice group, mentoring relationship, organization, or law firm. They repeatedly succumb to their perceptions of danger or discomfort and flee to a situation that they think will be safer or better without ever looking at their role in creating their perception or options for changing a situation.

Worksheet: Diagnosing Your Wanderer Tendencies

Review your résumé and identify each career transition. For each transition, answer the following questions:

1. Why did you make the transition?
2. How did your career change?
3. Did your goals or personal definition of success change? If so, how?
4. Did the transition bring you closer to one or more of your goals? Which ones?
5. Did the transition bring you closer to your personal definition of success?
6. If you have few transitions, have you attained many of your goals?
7. If you have few transitions, do you feel successful?

Interpreting Your Results

If your transitions, in general, brought you closer to a goal or to your personal definition for success or if they caused you to adjust your goals or personal definition of success, you have exhibited the right amount of Wanderer tendencies. If not, you might want to consider whether you have been using your Wanderer tendencies as a default reaction to challenges.

If you have few transitions and do not feel as though you have attained enough of your goals or been successful, you may not be using your Wanderer thinking enough.

§ 2:8   Changing the way you think about using power to address your challenges—The Magician

The power behind Magicians is a curiosity about themselves and their world that drives them toward a goal. They balance a sense of independent identity with a sense of being part of a larger whole through self-reflection, data collection and analysis, and intelligent experimentation. They see differences as the fertile ground necessary for innovation through collaboration. The Magician is able to see the opportunities in threats and to figure out how to leverage them for a strategic advantage. The need to have power over others, which we see as a safety or problem-solving mechanism in the Orphan, Martyr, and Warrior types, is replaced with peer relationships and a sense of equality in and appreciation of differences. This is most helpful when you are trying to identify your clients or employer's unexpressed or unknown wants and needs. What might they want and need if only they knew it existed?

This is an extraordinarily useful perspective for responding to the biases that make it difficult for some people to embrace or even accept differences. Differences are present because of the different social identity groups to which people belong and the different ways of thinking, seeing the world, and responding to challenges in the world that different people utilize. Curiosity is a critical skill to develop, especially for the exploratory conversations that are hallmarks of the best diversity and inclusion work within organizations.

Curiosity is an invaluable skill. Judge C. Darnell Jones II sits on the United States District Court for the Eastern District of Pennsylvania. He possesses a significant amount of formal power in that role, yet his curiosity may be one of his strongest assets. He is African American and has had his share of challenging experiences in Oklahoma, where he grew up, and in Philadelphia, where he now resides. The fact that he was a star football player and class president in high school and college or that he is a federal court judge today was not and is not enough privilege to overcome the racial bias that drives the reactions he has received from some people. His curiosity about why people behave the way that they do is a powerful tool for him. He shared the following story.

In the 1960s, when Judge Jones was a college student, he was a member of The Fellowship of Christian Athletes, a national social and religious organization for coaches and athletes. He was asked to speak about race relations at a parsonage in western Kansas on a Sunday afternoon. Sitting with him on chairs in a circle of approximately 20 people was a White farmer in overalls. Judge Jones remembers that the farmer said to him, "Mr. Jones, you sound like you're very educated and have really good manners. You're a well-mannered young man. One thing that I don't understand is that if you accept that the Bible says 'slaves

35

obey your masters,' don't you think you and your people should
still be slaves?" His natural curiosity about the experiences others have had that caused them to react in ways that are driven
by a deep racial bias enabled him to respond to that white man
in overalls with a statement of acceptance of that man as he was
and a request that the man accept Jones as he was. It diffused
the situation.

More recently, Judge Jones has found that making a maximum
effort to understand people helps him when, despite how well he
is dressed, he may still walk into a store and find the store owner
following him around or get stopped while driving his car.

The vulnerability of the Magician archetype is an excess of
distraction, ideas, diversity of thinking, and failed **Influence
Strategies** grounded in too much collaboration. There are times
where simple, clear direction would suffice and the Magician
archetype leads to chaos. Chaos is best managed with a constant
check on whether our actions are aligned with a clear purpose or
objective and the values that matter to us most. Curiosity, collaboration, and the necessary willingness to learn from mistakes
are also useful in business development efforts.

By all counts, Amy Schulman is a very successful and powerful
lawyer. According to the Pfizer Web site:[1]

> Ms. Schulman joined Pfizer in June 2008 and saw the company
> through its $68 billion acquisition of Wyeth. She led a major reor-
> ganization of the Legal Division to align with Pfizer's new business-
> unit structure and broadened its scope to include lawyers in all
> markets. In early 2009, she spearheaded the Pfizer Legal Alliance,
> an innovative approach to engaging outside counsel. She is
> recognized as a leading voice for transforming the billable-hour
> model and for redefining the value of legal services.

> Before coming to Pfizer, Ms. Schulman was a partner at DLA Piper,
> where she was a member of the Board and Executive Policy Com-
> mittees, and built and led the international law firm's mass tort
> and class-action practice. Her clients included GE Healthcare,
> Cisco, Wyeth, Philip Morris, Kraft Foods and Pfizer, for which she
> served as lead national counsel in multidistrict litigation involving
> pain medicines Bextra and Celebrex.

[Section 2:8]

[1]Amy Schulman bio. Pfizer Web site, http://www.pfizer.com/about/leadersh
ip__and__structure/leadership__executives__schulman.jsp (last visited March 4,
2010).

In September 2004, she was interviewed for the ABA on-line journal, Law Practice Today,[2] because of her position as a highly influential female rainmaker. In her interview, she spoke about the importance of self-reflection and a willingness to make mistakes. She said:

> [N]ot to be afraid to pick yourself up when you do something wrong and do it again, do it better, do it differently. When you drive to be perfect and yet recognize that no one is, it's important to be open to learning from your mistakes. I've had to learn that consciously. Many women are paralyzed because we are afraid to make a mistake.

While referencing the importance of finding "your own voice," a significant piece in any self-reflection, she explained her rainmaking success this way:

> My rainmaking success comes from two things: my conviction that I can be really helpful to clients and my ability to offer them a valuable service. Rainmaking sounds like you're selling something. What you have to want is not business, but what the business represents: to help clients with something they need done and can't do without you, or at least, not as easily.

First, Schulman told herself a story about resilience, tenacity, and a willingness to learn from mistakes. Second, she told herself a story about how to be influential that was in alignment with her identity and values of being "really helpful to clients" with "valuable service." This is not a Warrior's story about the power of conquest. It is a Magician's story of curiosity and collaboration; curiosity about how to be really helpful to clients and collaboration with clients to deliver whatever the client thinks is a valuable service. Indeed, the words, she chose to describe herself were these: intense, thoughtful, optimistic, curious, relentless, and energetic.

Worksheet: Diagnosing Your Magician Tendencies

1. Explain how you have used your curiosity to advance your career or develop your business.
2. Explain how your relationships have helped you attain goals.
3. Explain how your relationships have helped you to feel successful.
4. Describe a time that you transformed a threat into an opportunity.
5. Chart the diversity in your networks.

---

[2]Law Practice Today, Meet the Rainmaker, http://apps.americanbar.org/lpm/lpt/articles/wr09041.html (last visited March 4, 2010).

6. Are you too easily distracted or feeling like there is too much chaos in your life?

Interpreting Your Results

If you struggled to answer questions 1 to 4, you may need to develop your Magician archetype. If so, is there enough diversity in your networks? For example, if you are interested in developing new clients, you should be active in networks and organizations that are frequented by people who have the necessary decision-making power or referral power. If your firm does mostly local work in a niche area for national law firms, then you need to be active in the networks frequented by the decision-makers in the national law firms. If you continue to meet people who cannot or will not refer you work, then you need to expand your network.

Pearson's archetypes are the stories that people tell themselves about responding to challenges and moving closer to their goals and personal definitions of success. Most people rely on one or two of these archetypal behaviors more heavily than the others, especially in times of stress. People tend to ignore problems, rely only on themselves, fight to the death, ignore their own wants, needs, and expectations, leave a bad situation, or look for an innovative solution. Ideally, one should learn to develop and balance a variety of possible responses to challenges, pulling out the responses most appropriate for the situation. Learning about the thought processes that one tends to use without thinking opens up choices of approaching challenges strategically, which increases the likelihood that a person will be successful in addressing his or her challenges.

Worksheet: Writing Your Hero's Journey Stories

1. Write a story describing your biggest personal challenge and how you responded to it.
2. Write a story describing your biggest professional challenge and how you responded to it.
3. Write a story describing one of your current career goals, the biggest challenge associated with it, and how you intend to respond.
4. For each story, identify the archetypes involved and describe your perceptions and actions in terms of power and vulnerabilities.
5. Self-reflection: How are your thoughts and actions affected by the following:
   a. The stories you are telling yourself?
   b. The stories we are telling ourselves as a society?
   c. The stories we are telling ourselves as lawyers (a group within society)?

6. What are the six words that best describe you?

Worksheet: Archetypes and Personal Experiences

My Experiences with the Archetypes

Archetype	Distinctive Elements	Experiences with Archetype in Others	Feelings When I Notice It in Others	Examples of Archetype Expressed in Self	Feelings When I Express Archetype

After filling in the table, answer the following questions:

1. Which elements of any archetype would you like to develop further in yourself?
2. What would you like to change in your reactions to any archetype?
3. What would you like to change in your expression of any archetype?

§ 2:9 Digging deeper—Emotional reactions to power and influence

The sooner one abandons the idea that pure, rational, logical thought exits, the sooner one will be ready to learn how to manage and use emotions effectively.

> The notion that there is 'pure thought,' rationality devoid of feeling, is a fiction, an illusion based on inattention to the subtle moods that follow us through the day. We have feelings about everything we do, think about, imagine, remember. Thought and feeling are inextricably woven together.[1]

In addition to having default thinking about challenges, people have default feelings about challenges, power, and influence. The lawyers interviewed for this book were asked what they thought and felt when they heard or saw the words power and influence. Interestingly, almost everyone pitted the two words against each other by defining one in terms of something the other was not. Power was often, but not each time, cast in the bad role and influence in the good role. The table below shows the battle that was set up between the two words.

Power	Influence
Force	Convince
Abuse	More of a good thing
Ability to get things done	Weaker, help to get things done, but will not guarantee outcome
Military might	Feelings will influence others
Make the decision and have it implemented	Able to convince others with power to make the correct decision and implement it
To change things, get things done, positive thinking	Negative, undue, improper peddling

If a person has set up a false dichotomy with the two concepts, it is important to transform power and influence from an antagonistic relationship into a synergistic one. The antagonistic relationship may lead to a values-based conflict, while a synergistic relationship makes it more comfortable to develop and expand **Power Bases** and **Influence Strategies**. For instance a person who does not value military might and highly values feelings as a way of responding to a challenge is likely to avoid using the Warrior behaviors or will use them less effectively even if the situation calls for that means of conflict resolution because "[t]o seek power even for sincere and honorable reasons, [might place that

---

[Section 2:9]

[1]Daniel Goleman. Working with Emotional Intelligence 52 (1998).

person] in a value contradiction."[2] People who perceive power as a limited resource, an aggression, or a defense to aggression are likely to home in on "how to neutralize, combat, or defend against it"[3] to create an effective shield against the power of others. This is the classic risk management perspective of an attorney and may be a highly effective perspective in that particular role. It may also diminish the role of an in-house attorney on a team, whose task is to find a way to structure a deal that the client wants or needs. If one only is able to identify the risks, it becomes very difficult to do anything but avoid them.

People attach strong emotions and beliefs to power and influence. Logically, water, food, and air are absolutely necessary for people to survive and thrive. These nouns evoke less highly charged emotional reactions than power and influence, which are equally necessary for people to survive and thrive. Indeed, without power, it is impossible to obtain and use water, food, and air to survive and thrive. Even breathing air, which is an unconscious physical act, requires lung power. One's emotional reaction to power and influence will affect that person's ability to notice and use his or her own **Power Bases** and **Influence Strategies**.

Jane Dalton's passion is encouraging young women to believe in themselves and succeed, as they have defined success for themselves. She thinks "power is wonderful. It needs to be respected and used wisely, but the more the better." Upon reflection of how feelings have changed over the years, she adds that when she was younger, she "would more likely have been afraid of power, because [she] did not think [she] had it."

One's beliefs and feelings about power and influence unconsciously affect one's decisions about whether and how to use power and **Influence Strategies** to enhance business development efforts and advance one's career in a two-part process. These two processes are pattern recognition and emotional tagging.

First, pattern recognition is primarily an unconscious process of perception through "the assembly of interpretations from many different parts of the brain [and] the filling in of gaps to produce an understanding." The brain "looks for a memory of past inputs that match . . . and makes assumptions about missing bits of in-

---

[2]B. Scott & P. van den Herik. Exercising Power in Organizations 40 OD Practitioner 29–35 (2008).

[3]Robert J. Marshak. Covert Processes at Work 148 (2008).

formation, and arrives at a point of view."[4] Pattern recognition is the reason why any of the archetypes explained earlier resonated with you. Pattern recognition is a process that leads to an interpretation of challenging moments and a decision of how to respond. Pattern recognition is sense making by estimating reality based upon memories of similar patterns. A person must go through that step before reaching a decision-making step. It is especially difficult to make sense of something that is innovative; i.e., new and creative, which by definition is very different from anything existing in a person's stored memories.

If your goal is to influence a group of people to adopt an innovative idea, expect resistance and develop a strategy to move past it. It is important to know how you react emotionally to using power and influence.

A senior policy analyst, and also a lawyer, at a large public construction agency (the "**Influencer**"), believed that the decision-making with regard to some issues faced by the agency would improve with research on aspects of the broader system and specific data from the municipality. The method to investigate these systemic issues depended on convincing various stakeholders of the feasibility of an innovative idea that was not yet crystallized. The **Influencer** began meeting with academics at various local institutions and with practitioners at the agency and at other construction agencies within the municipality to explore possibilities. That iterative process led to the creation of a systemic action research program that encompassed the systemic issues and partnered with academics from relevant disciplines, who do not typically work directly with government employees. Those government practitioners encountered the issues "on the ground."

Influencing people within large institutions to support an innovative idea and getting them to work together collaboratively on that innovative idea are challenges. The way that the **Influencer** thought about and responded to a evolving challenges directly affected the ability of the program to get off the ground. She first "crystallized the idea" and then "leveraged [her] position within a network of relationships to develop the program." In her words, she "just went for it." She was "flexible in all approaches, using everything and everyone to make connections." She was "fearless in speaking to complete strangers [and] quite aware that [she] might have sounded like a lunatic to some people, but [she] needed to start and eventually [her] idea resonated and

---

[4]Sydney Finkelstein, Jo Whitehead, and Andrew Campbell. Think Again 8 (2008).

[she] built upon the relationships with those who 'got it'." Equally important, she "used criticisms of the nascent idea" to continually restructure the explanation of the developing program to increase the chances of getting the necessary buy-in. This is how to "build a buzz" as that term is used in media relations and get an innovative idea the support it needs to become more than an idea. It is more difficult to influence people to support an idea that is unlike anything else stored in their memories, arguably, because of the process of pattern recognition. It takes enough confidence with one's approach to a challenge to use power in an effective and iterative **Influence Strategy** and not give up too early.

In the second process, emotional tagging, "we tag our thoughts and memories with emotions. These tags, when triggered by a pattern recognition match, tell us whether to pay attention to something or ignore it, and they give us an action orientation."[5] Without emotions we are unable to take an "action orientation." Simply put, we are stuck, stopped in our tracks, without the power of emotions. We may justify our decisions with reason and logic, but we make them emotionally. Let's consider a real-world example of this phenomenon in a person who was part of a group traditionally defined by their ability to set aside their emotions and make decisions rationally and logically—lawyers.

Dr. Anthonio Damasio is an internationally recognized leader in neuroscience, whose research has shown that "emotions play a central role in social cognition and decision-making."[6] Damasio treated a highly successful corporate lawyer who had a small tumor in his prefrontal lobes, which was removed with surgery. The surgeon inadvertently severed the connection between the prefrontal lobes and the amygdala, the center for feeling and processing emotions. Although the lawyer had no discernible cognitive deficits, he lost his ability to make even the simplest decisions, like when to schedule an appointment, despite his ability to provide a rational argument of the pros and cons of each possible time slot.[7] Emotions enable us to make decisions.

Emotions enable people to make decisions and sometimes they interfere with one's ability to make good decisions. It is helpful to know why we feel something, what we feel, and when we feel it. It has been hypothesized that most people are influenced by: 1. a

---

[5]Sydney Finkelstein, Jo Whitehead, and Andrew Campbell. Think Again 9 (2008).

[6]http://www.usc.edu/programs/neuroscience/faculty/profile.php?fid=27 (last visited February 20, 2011).

[7]Daniel Goleman. Working with Emotional Intelligence 52 (1998).

need to be liked; 2. a need to set personal goals and achieve them; and/or 3. a need for power—the influencing of others.[8] Many lawyers appear to be driven by a need to achieve personal goals as exemplified by Carrie Hogan. Goals are necessary, but they are not sufficient. Emotions that are triggered also have the potential to interfere with one's ability to make a decision that will bring a person closer to his or her goals, happiness, and personal definition of success. That reason and the fact that emotions are contagious suggest the importance of learning how to identify and manage one's emotions. The contagious nature of emotions is explained in the next chapter.

Case Study: Sheryl Axelrod—From Big Firm to Entrepreneur with an Idea of Success and by Managing Emotions

Sheryl Axelrod, President-Elect of the Temple Law Alumni Association, practiced law for 14 years before starting her own law firm in Philadelphia. Her firm is a state-certified, woman-owned, three-attorney firm. Before starting the firm, she had moved from law firm to law firm. She loved the people she worked with and the work she got, she just never found the right fit. She felt she tried everything, from practicing in very small firms to very large ones:

> I was never truly satisfied with my situation until I created it. I spent years trying to align what was best for whatever firm I was in with what was best for me. I worked for the greater good of the firm and my friends in it, and while I got a certain satisfaction out of enhancing the place, at some point I realized that I wanted more than what was best for the firms. I wanted to be the one deciding the direction of the firm. I wanted to choose how my cases would be handled. I wanted to be at the helm.

The realization was simultaneously exciting and terrifying for her. She was solely responsible for paying her mortgage and car payments. There was a tremendous amount of uncertainty in the first steps of the transition because she could not ask clients whether they would remain loyal to her or the law firm she was leaving.

She built the motivation and courage to make the transition by seeing it as an opportunity to find satisfaction in practicing law the way that would make her happy and feel successful. She managed her fear of failing by considering the alternative, certain dissatisfaction in her career if she did not attempt to realize her

---

[8]D.C. McClelland and D.H. Burnham. Power is the Great Motivator (2003) Reprint RO301J Harvard Business Review Best of HR 1976.

dream. She said that she will never forget the day she gave notice. "I went up to my boss and said I was going to leave, I was going to start a new firm. Although I had practiced the speech, I was shaking when I gave it, but I knew deep down, it was a change I had to make."

She opened her own law firm and "luckily, almost every client I asked to come with me did," she said. "I hadn't realized then what I know now: it's all about relationships. My clients knew me. For the past four-plus years, they called me when they had a problem. They didn't think of the firm as their attorneys. They thought of me as their attorney. It was the best move I ever made."

Sheryl knew what happiness and success meant to her personally. She had a goal and effectively managed her emotions to move past the limitations of the Warrior and Martyr archetypes, while leveraging their strengths and also tapped into the benefits of a Wander. She embraced a Kierkegaardian leap of faith that she would be able to pay her bills because enough clients would want to maintain their relationship with her.

Worksheet: Emotional Awareness

Answer the following questions to assess your ability to recognize your emotions and manage their effects:

1. What is your process for noticing your emotional state, identifying the emotion, and identifying the triggering event?
2. Are you aware of the links between your feelings, thoughts, actions, and words?
3. Do you recognize the connection between your feelings and your performance?
4. What do you do to keep aware of your values and goals and use them for guidance?
5. How do you define power and influence? What emotions and images are embedded in those definitions?
6. Have you infused any values into the ways that you think about power or influence?
7. Have you infused any part of your identity into the ways that you think about power or influence?

Assessment tools are a useful means for developing self-awareness about how one thinks and feels about challenges, conflict, power, and influence. The Myers Briggs Type Indicator®

("MBTI®")[9] examines preferences for noticing and gathering data and making decisions about data, the Firo B considers one's expressed and wanted levels of inclusion, control, and affection, and the Thomas-Kilmann Conflict Mode Instrument ("TKI")[10] considers a person's relative preferences for noticing conflict and responding to it. The use of tools in workshops offers the additional opportunity to discover and observe how others think, feel, and behave.

§ 2:10   Chapter summary

- The perception of conflict or a challenge triggers the need to use power and influence.
- One's default reaction to challenges affects one's ability to think and act intentionally and strategically. Identifying one's default reactions and developing an awareness of other possible reactions expands one's ability to think and act intentionally and strategically.
- Dr. Carol Pearson's model offers six archetypes to use to identify and expand one's thinking about and responses to a challenge.
- Decision-making, including decisions about whether and how to use power and influence, results from two processes: pattern recognition and emotional tagging. Pattern recognition is a process of estimating reality from similar memories. Tagging one's estimates of reality with emotions drives decision-making. Thus, it is important to identify the emotions that are driving your decisions about your use of power and influence.

---

[9]The MBTI® and its usefulness is explained in detail in § 5:3.

[10]The TKI and its usefulness is explained in detail in § 5:8.

Chapter 3

How Decisions Are Made

KeyCite®: Cases and other legal materials listed in KeyCite Scope can be researched through the KeyCite service on Westlaw®. Use KeyCite to check citations for form, parallel references, prior and later history, and comprehensive citator information, including citations to other decisions and secondary materials.

---

§ 3:1   Chapter focus and questions

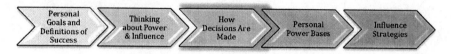

Influence Strategies are designed to affect a **Target's** thinking and decision-making. Two people that I interviewed, Gary Levin and Jane Dalton, separately said that they are aware of how easy it is to assume that other people think and make decisions the way that they do and have learned to check their assumptions. As Gary said, he has also realized that it is easy to read one's own motives into others' decisions and to guard against projecting one's motives and fears. Effective **Influence Strategies** are designed with an understanding of how other people make decisions. Additionally, an **Influencer** benefits from knowing something about how decisions happen in a system, organization, and group. The last chapter explained the different lenses an **Influencer** might use by default when responding to a challenge and the roles that pattern recognition and emotions play in decision making and behavior. This chapter includes models for diagnosing power within any system to determine where the decision making power exists and how it will be exercised. A system is simply an interconnected set of groups and/or individuals that is organized for a purpose. This chapter also includes a model for identifying the motivators or blockers that affect the decision-making processes of individuals.

To fully analyze how decisions are made, it is necessary to: (1) identify who has the decision-making power that will impact the **Influencer's** goals, (2) determine how the decision-making power will be exercised, and (3) consider the points of influencing the individuals with the power. First, within the **Influencer's Target** system, organization, or group, who has the decision-making power over the decisions that matter to the **Influencer**? This is not always obvious and in fact may be contrary to what appears in an organizational chart. Second, if the decision-making power rests within a particular group, what decision-making processes will that group use? Third, how will the individuals with decision-making power be motivated to or blocked from making the decisions desired by the **Influencer**?

Questions:

- How can you determine who in a system has the power exists to make a particular decision?
- How do you determine the type of political power controlling an individual or group?
- What are the different ways in which individuals might be influenced in their decision making?

§ 3:2   Diagnosing power in systems

Influencing a person or a group in a large organization typically depends on getting "buy-in" from different stakeholders. One is often not able to make decisions alone in an organization; thus, "influencing skills are a must and one must be willing to work with people to exchange thoughts, bring forward ideas, and impact change in that fashion. In a large corporation, it is the essence of the job," according to Ritva Sotamaa.

A system is an interconnected set of groups and/or individuals that is organized for a purpose. Understanding power dynamics in systems is a critical skill for influencing the decision-making in any system. The universe is a system, as is a university. The purpose can be intentional or not and long-term or short-lived. One purpose of a university is to educate its students. An ecosystem's purpose is to support life through a natural and interconnected set of elements. Some groups are formed to address a particular problem within an organization and once solved, the group disbands.

Systems come in all sizes and can be nested in one another. An organization, like a university, is a system that is part of a larger social system—the higher education system. Systems have boundaries that arise from place, time, or purpose. It helps to think of nesting systems by size so that an individual is within a group that is part of an organization, which is nested within a larger social system. Effective **Influence Strategies** are designed with an understanding of which groups alone or in conjunction with one another, within a **Target** organization, will make the decisions that matter to the **Influencer's** goals.

Individual • Group • Organization • System

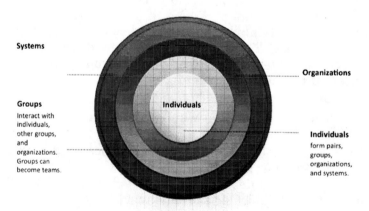

Decision making in organizations depends on the location of power and that depends on the political dynamics. Power can be at any hierarchical level of the organization or diffused throughout.

Regardless of the type of system in which a person works, it is important to know who owns the power to make the decisions that matter to that person's career aspirations. A person interested in developing business from any organization similarly needs to know who controls the power to make the decisions regarding choice of lawyers or firms. A lot of time is wasted trying to influence people and groups who do not have the power to make the decisions that matter to an **Influencer's** goals.

Figuring out who, individually or as part of a group, has the power to make the decisions that matter to one's goals starts with examining the formal structure of a **Target** organization or group, but the reality is that in most organizations the informal power structures or networks tell the true story of decision making. Determine who has informal power in a group or organization by observation and asking questions about who actually makes the decisions. An **Influencer** should also determine who, within the **Target** organization, is sought after for information, permission, and/or as a trusted advisor for the type of decisions that matter to the **Influencer**.

In addition to figuring out who has the power to make these important decisions, it is critical for an **Influencer** to figure out how he or she is connected to that person or group. Understanding one's networks, power, and one's place within those networks matters.

MAPPING YOUR NETWORKS

Most Powerful People or Groups: Who are they? Which departments are then in? What committees are they on? What resources do they control? Who do they listen to?

Key People and Groups: Who is connected to the most powerful people and groups and how?

You: How are you connected to Key People and Groups and Most Powerful People and Groups? What could you do to improve these connections?

Worksheet: Network Organization Map

Create a network organization map, the purpose of which is to find out who has the power to make the decisions that need to be made in your favor. To do this, collect data from the following written documents and sources:

- Organizational charts
- Job descriptions
- Formal titles
- Committee assignments
- Compensation policies
- Qualifications for career advancement or work assignments

Observe and ask questions about the following:

- Who decides the strategic goals for the group or organization?
- How do people act toward and speak with each other? Who seems to be well-supported by others in the organization? Who appears to have influence over whom? Who speaks to whom with respect? Who speaks to whom with condescension? Who defers to whom and who treats whom like a peer? Where do you fit in with the power dynamics?[1]
- Which departments are large, profitable, and seem to have a greater portion of the budget and number of promotions?
- Who has power because of belonging to a particular social group? For example, does graduating from a particular college or law school put a person in a powerful network of connections?

§ 3:3 All organizations are political: Political dynamics and decision making

Organizations are systems of government; they are "intrinsically political."[1] Governmental agencies, law schools, large corporations, not-for-profit agencies, industry groups, professional associations, and small businesses are organizations. Nearly everyone who wants to advance his or her career or develop business is connected to an organization professionally. The only people who are not connected are those isolated in their work and

---

[Section 3:2]

[1]Larry E. Greiner and Virginia E. Schein. Power and Organization Development 84–91 (1988).

[Section 3:3]

[1]Gareth Morgan. Images of Organizations 149–206 (2006).

those who never need anything from anyone who is connected to an organization. In organizations, sometimes the political dynamics that matter most are not the most apparent. Informal networks are much more influential, and in ways that are more difficult to track than the less powerful formal hierarchy.

Political dynamics privilege the interests of certain individuals and groups over others. It is impossible to understand diversity and inclusion without understanding political dynamics. The ability to successfully implement any strategic initiative within or involving any organization depends on understanding the organization's political dynamics. This means that a person who wants to advance her or his position within an organization or wants to obtain business from an organization must understand the **Target** organization's political dynamics.

Political dynamics shape negotiations and mediations and they create and maintain order among the members of the organization. Maintaining order among members is affected by the development, maintenance, and alteration of the relationships between and among the organization members. Advancing an **Influencer's** formal position within his or her organization will involve negotiations by the **Influencer** and others on behalf of the **Influencer.** Advancing anyone in the organization reorders all of the other members of the organization. When a client gives a particular matter to a particular lawyer or firm that it had not previously used, it reorders the client's legal vendors and their respective relationships with the client.

Political dynamics are about relationships between people who have differing amounts of power to make different decisions within the organization and who have different interests, i.e., wants, needs, and expectations. Knowing how a particular organization assigns power to shape action requires knowing whose interests are at stake and the relationships that protect those interests. That's politics.

Political dynamics are responsible for the fact that you are more likely to receive good evaluations and promotions from a person who hired you than from one who inherited you.[2] The people who have hired you have an interest in proving their competence to others by showing that hiring you was a good decision.

Knowing who has power is important. Knowing the type of power an individual or group has is also important. There are six different types of political power dynamics that might be present in any organization. They might be present at the highest levels

---

[2]Jeffrey Pfeffer, Power 23 (2010).

of the organization or within a particular practice group, department, or division. An **Influencer** must analyze the dynamics at all levels that affect his or her ability to attain goals and decide whether attaining those goals depends on developing a particular type of power personally, influencing the political dynamics in existence, or waiting until the dynamics dissipate. The six types of power possibly at play within any organization are: Autocratic, Bureaucratic, Technocratic or Expert, Codetermination, Representative Democracy, and Direct Democracy.

§ 3:4 All organizations are political: Political dynamics and decision making—Autocratic power

In an Autocracy, the power resides in a single person or small group that controls resources. The person or group with this type of power has risen to this privileged role because of tradition, charisma, or control over resources. Rainmakers with control over significant clients are one example. Professors with significant funding are another example. Judges in their own courtroom controlling the process of a trial are yet another example. A fourth example is the managing partner, who, because of tradition, has been chosen to lead. At Jones Day, the current managing partner chooses his successor; although the partnership has the power to vote out the managing partner, it has never happened. The managing partner is the only person with a formal title and the person who decides on the compensation for each partner. His decision is based on information provided by an 11-member advisory committee, selected by the managing partner. This is an example of an autocracy, which receives high praise from the partners there.[1] It is also an autocracy that promotes many women to positions as office managing partners.[2]

Do you need to influence someone who possesses this kind of political power to achieve your goals? For example, if you want to do the work of a particular client or be involved in a particular client presentation, you need an action plan to influence the partner with the client relationship to include you. If you want to implement a particular program at your law firm and that decision rests with a single managing partner, you need an action

---

[Section 3:4]

[1]Amanda Royal. Jones Day Keeps its Paychecks Private. http://www.law.com/jsp/article.jsp?id=1202465019083 (last visited on November 22, 2010).

[2]Metropolitan Corporate Counsel. Jones Day Forges a New Path in Boston http://www.metrocorpcounsel.com/current.php?artType=view&artMonth=March&artYear=2011&EntryNo=11897 (last visited March 20, 2011).

plan to influence that person to let you lead a task force to implement the program. These are examples of autocratic dynamics. Accomplishing goals that depend upon your successfully navigating autocratic dynamics means finding out what the person in control wants or needs as a condition of supporting the decisions that need to be made in your favor. Learn as much as possible about what motivates this person to do anything. Gather data from others and directly from the person by asking him or her. Do not complain that there are no written guidelines; in these instances that is not where the critical power resides.

§ 3:5 All organizations are political: Political dynamics and decision making—Bureaucratic power

Bureaucratic power resides in the written rules, policies, or procedures. Think of the power derived from a partnership agreement or evaluation and compensation procedures. Do you need to know more about the bureaucracy in your organization or your client organization? What requirements or obstacles are presented in the written agreements, policies, and/or procedures? For example, if you want a certain level of compensation, what are the written standards that you are required to meet? If you want to become the managing partner of your firm, what is the procedure to follow? If you want to serve on a particular committee, what is the process? If you want to become a judge within the state court system, what do you need to do? If you want to advance to the next level within your organization, what are the performance requirements? What are the standards, if any, for becoming an equity partner or getting the work assignments that you want? Bureaucratic power is often one power dynamic to consider; however, frequently there are also others present.

§ 3:6 All organizations are political: Political dynamics and decision making—Technocratic or expert power

Technocratic power is similar to autocratic power, but it is a consequence of one's expert ability to solve relevant problems. If you want a new video conferencing system to link your offices together, chances are that great deference will be given to the opinion of the law firm's Information Technology director. Lawyers with true expert power in the marketplace find that their services are price insensitive. There are two parts to this expertise. It is one that few others have and which is in high demand.

In a law firm, technocratic power generally creates the ability to charge one's clients without the downward market pressure we see attached to commodity work. Is there a particular client need that only you can fulfill because of your expertise or some other factor, like the process for delivery or additional deep value? Is there an expertise you ought to develop so that you are positioning yourself for the vesting of technocratic power?

§ 3:7 All organizations are political: Political dynamics and decision making—The power of codetermination

Codetermination decision-making is a configuration that places power in a coalition comprising opposing political interests. Coalition members know that they answer to their constituents and that any decision may require compromise. Have you been told that getting permission to do what you want is dependent on whether several people will agree? A firm which is governed by a committee or group comprising people from various factions or cliques within the firm is an example of codetermination dynamics. Your best option is to convince the various people individually to support your request. Otherwise, you risk convincing fewer people than you need for a favorable vote. I have seen a person from one faction convince only the faction leader, who then is unable to convince the leaders of the other factions. I've also seen conflict-adverse members of a coalition avoid discussion and deciding critical issues and thereby cause stagnation.

§ 3:8 All organizations are political: Political dynamics and decision making—The power of a representative democracy

In a Representative Democracy, power rests in those elected to office for a specified period of time. When the time is up, so is the power. Time is a factor to consider if the power dynamics are presently unfavorable to your interests. Running for office is another possible option. Voting someone out of office is yet another option.

§ 3:9 All organizations are political: Political dynamics and decision making—The power and problems with a direct democracy

Finally, in a direct democracy, power rests in everyone equally. Decisions may result from a simple majority, an agreed-upon higher percentage, or unanimous vote. In many law firms, this leads to slow decision-making or an inability to make decisions at all. If you have attended meetings as an equity partner, where each partner has a single vote and it seems impossible to make any decision, you have experienced first-hand the downside to direct democracy dynamics. Since everyone has an equal vote, nobody has sufficient power on his or her own. Skills in effective listening, empathy, strategic communication, negotiation, and mediation become extremely important.

Summary of Political Dynamics

Autocracy	• Single person or small group • Controls resources
Bureaucracy	• Documents • Rules, Policies, Procedures
Technocracy	• Expert with Unique Skills
Codetermination	• Group • Coalition of Opposing Interest Bases
Representative Democracy	• Elected Officials • Time Limit
Direct Democracy	• 1 person 1 vote

It is likely that more than one political dynamic will affect the decisions that matter to you. Do not stop your analysis of the political dynamics the moment you notice the presence of a single dynamic. Use the following as a template for creating an appropriate action plan, which is sensitive to any political dynamics that will influence the outcome:

Worksheet: Political Dynamics and Action Planning

What is your goal? _____

You will need to identify all goals and for each ask the following questions:

1. What is your action plan, i.e., your specific implementation steps to achieve the goal?
2. For any implementation step, is political power an issue?
3. If so, which type(s) of political power?
4. What is your action plan to address the specific political dynamics? Do you need or want the power? Do you need the help of someone who has the power?
5. Add the necessary details to your implementation steps depending upon how you answered the prior questions. Consider the implementation steps to be a process of intelligent experimentation and be prepared to revise as necessary.

Organizations will generally use mixed types of power dynamics; although they may lean more strongly toward one type. As you design, implement, and revise your goal-oriented action plans, identify the various political dynamics that are present and will continue to impact your ability to successfully implement your plan. Adjust your action plan as needed. Keep in mind that the best strategy, which is exactly what an action plan is, is constantly revised.

§ 3:10 Individuals and decision making: How can you influence the decision making of empowered individuals?

Effective **Influence Strategies** identify the individuals or groups that have decision-making power, the type of power they possess, and the possible points in an individual's decision-making process that are susceptible to influence. This section explains the various points that are susceptible to influence. Whether individuals are acting within a group or individually, there appears to be an order to the decision-making process. People collect information from their environment. They have an unconscious emotional reaction. They behave in a way that is aligned with their emotional reaction. Then they become conscious of the feelings that are driving their behavior. Finally, they become able to make a decision using a logical reasoning process.[1] The emotional and rational influences on one's decision making are closely connected. Chapter 2 explained the impact of one's emotions on one's choice of when and how to use power and influence. This chapter explains the effect that emotions have on a **Target's** decision making.

There are six overt and covert dimensions of organizational change.[2] Intentional organizational change is influencing organizations, which comprise groups and individuals. The dimensions of organizational change are also lenses to view the points at which an individual's decision making can be influenced. The model below summarizes the various points of influence to consider as part of designing an effective **Influence Strategy.**

Motivators or Blockers: Points of Influence in Decision Making

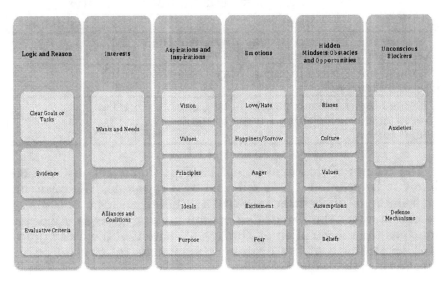

[Section 3:10]

[1]Sydney Finkelstein, Jo Whitehead, and Andrew Campbell. Think Again 37 (2008).

[2]Robert J. Marshak. Covert Processes at Work 15 (2006).

§ 3:11 Individuals and decision making: How can you influence the decision making of empowered individuals?—Logic and reason

Lawyers privilege the use of logic and reason in decision-making. This is rationality-based persuasion, or "trying to influence someone's attitudes, beliefs, or actions by offering reasons and/or evidence to justify a proposal on its merits."[1] There are myriad courses and books for lawyers who are interested in honing this particular type of **Influence Strategy**. It is at the heart of what lawyers do when they are acting in their lawyer role.

Let's look closer at reason and logic. How objective is it? It is not surprising that a person is more likely to respond favorably to a request for a favor if he or she is given a reason to do so. What is surprising is that even an obvious and expected reason works. Compare the results of the compliance rate with the three requests in the experiment, summarized below.[2]

Framing a Request and Compliance Rates

Request	% Compliance
"Excuse me, I have 5 pages. May I use the Xerox machine because I'm in a rush?"	94%
"Excuse me, I have 5 pages. May I use the Xerox machine?"	60%
"Excuse me, I have 5 pages. May I use the Xerox machine because I have to make some copies?"	93%

The results of this experiment suggest that a request is more likely to be granted if it is followed by a rationale. The structure or framing of an **Influence Strategy** based on logic and reason seems to affect the **Target's** decision-making process almost as much as the reason offered. The actual content of the communication or strength of the argument wasn't as influential as the structure of the request.

The process of using logic and reason to evaluate possibilities has three components: (1) the options that the **Target** will consider; (2) the evidence in support or against each option; and (3) the evaluative model or criteria used to decide on an option.

[Section 3:11]

[1] G. Richard Shell and Mario Moussa. The Art of Woo 37 (2007).

[2] Robert B. Cialdini, Ph.D. Influence: The Psychology of Persuasion 4 (1984).

Even jurors in a trial, although given a model for making their decision (the jury instructions) and the evidence to use in that model, consciously or unconsciously decide how to interpret the model and the weight to give each piece of evidence. Influence points in this logic and reason process include the model, the interpretation of the model, the evidence, and the interpretation of the evidence.

§ 3:12 Individuals and decision making: How can you influence the decision making of empowered individuals?—Interests

When the interests of various individuals or groups drive the decision making process, the shifting needs and wants of the various decision-makers and their constituencies have a significant influence on the outcome of any discussion. An example of competing interests is when each of two departments in a law firm wants to advance its own associate to partner and there is only one spot available. The outcome may depend on forming alliances and trading promises or other favors with anyone who has voting power. Even if the only need is to influence a person not to argue with a decision, understanding that person's interests in the nature of political pressures helps.

Steven Stein Cushman routinely faces that challenge. He often must tell people that they can't have something that they want or need or that they can't do something that they want to do. The people he tells then have to report the bad news back to their bosses. He uses a strategy of talking to agency counsel or contracting officers about how they can present an answer or position that is contrary to what their bosses want to hear. He understands and takes into account their interests and needs as he influences them to become more accepting of an unpalatable answer to their request. He includes in his answer an explanation for them to use. "A lot of these people are under a lot of pressure from their commissioners. It creates a lot of stress to go back and say the answer is 'no.' You want to be able to help them." Helping them strengthens relationships and also helps him.

When Ritva knows that she has to promote an issue that she thinks might be controversial, she engages the various stakeholders in discussions well in advance of the time a decision will be made. She wants to understand the general mood about the issue of the various stakeholders. She wants to build momentum for the issue and also learn in advance where the impediments lay and the wisest way to move the issue forward.

§ 3:13   Individuals and decision making: How can you influence the decision making of empowered individuals?—Aspirations and inspirations

An aspiration is a desire to achieve something. An inspiration is a feeling of enthusiasm that leads to ideas to do something. A person might aspire to develop into a lawyer with an outstanding reputation for a high level of expertise. After hearing the managing partner of a particular law firm talk about the opportunities at that firm, that person might be inspired and conclude that if she or he joins the managing partner's firm she or he will be able to work with the best lawyers and on the most interesting projects in the field and develop the professional reputation that the person aspires to achieve. Both aspirations and inspirations are points of influence. Influencing a decision by inspiration is "focus-[ing] on the ideas . . . hopes for the future . . . people's personal goals with a meaningful vision."[1]

A government lawyer explained her decision making process this way, "For most of my career, the majority of what I've done is related to changing some aspect of the world that makes sense to me [based on my] personal viewpoint about what's the right thing to do . . . aligned with [my] view of morality and personal values." She is able to use this motivation to create the conditions to lead teams effectively. She defines a strategy, figures out the skill set of each person, and tailors job responsibilities to their strengths. She encourages collaboration across unit lines, which creates the interdependency of team members with different skills sets, and supports learning new things to broaden skill sets. Since their day-to-day responsibilities depend on the "news cycle," the ideal team members are motivated by a vision and an adrenaline rush. If you want to influence someone like this particular lawyer, gather as much information as possible about his or her personal vision, values, ideals, and principles.

C. Lash Harrison, is the first and only managing partner of the employment law firm of Ford & Harrison, LLP. Harrison has led the firm from 14 lawyers to close to 190 and is inspiring attorneys at his firm to become mentors and champions of attorneys who might otherwise be overlooked. Harrison says:

> [W]e all need mentors and champions . . . We want to make sure that we don't overlook the fact that minority attorneys sometimes

---

[Section 3:13]

[1]Daniel Goleman, Richard Boyatzis, and Annie McKee. Primal Leadership 212 (2002).

aren't comfortable reaching out and trying to establish those relationships. It can be hard, because in most firms in America still, most partners are white. [He talks about developing programs for attorneys that are] investments for the long term . . . you hope that it will allow people to be more successful, and if they are, the firm will be too.[2]

He inspires by telling people that the firm will be more successful if they invest time in all of their talent. He also taps into the value of social justice within their firm culture by reminding people that there is not racial equity at the partnership level of most law firms in the United States.

Inspiration is a lever for changing someone's behavior, but it alone may be enough only to build energy for making a change. Without more, like knowing the steps to take to bring about a particular change, it may be ineffective to attain the intended outcome.

§ 3:14 Individuals and decision making: How can you influence the decision making of empowered individuals?—Emotions

People react to their environment emotionally and then make a decision, which they align with their emotional reactions.[1] Superimpose the fact that emotions are contagious.[2] Emotions direct a significant step in the decision-making process, yet their presence often remains completely hidden to many people. Once a person makes a decision, that person tags that decision with a simple positive or negative emotion for future reference. This means that one's present emotions also dictate one's future decisions and actions. If a person concludes that a situation is similar to a past experience, the person will pull up the past decision with its emotional tagging and use it as a guide for the present

---

[2]Nick Brown. Innovative Managing Partner: C. Lash Harrison. Law 360 from: http://topnews.law360.com/print__article/176366 (last visited June 21, 2010).

[Section 3:14]

[1]Sydney Finkelstein, Jo Whitehead, and Andrew Campbell. Think Again 37 (2008).

[2]Alison L. Hill, David G. Rand, Martin A. Nowak, and Nicholas A. Christakis. Emotions as Infectious Disease in a Large Social Network: the SISa Model. Proceedings of the Royal Society Publishing: http://rspb.royalsocietypubl ishing.org/content/early/2010/07/03/rspb.2010.1217.full (last visited November 16, 2010).

decision making.[3] The stronger the emotional tag, like vivid events, personal experiences, or easily imagined events, the more likely the memory will be used for comparison.[4] This may form the basis for excluding a potential juror during a jury selection process.

In contrast, information conveyed as a story or as materials to be studied and learned is not marked with an equally strong tag and not as "available." The consequence is that "an experience can influence our thinking more than it should because of its availability."[5] Adults learn better through personal experiences than by reading or lecture alone. This is the reason that attending workshops, joining peer leadership groups, and using coaches are so important for anyone who wants to develop and expand his or her **Power Bases** and **Influence Strategies**.

Emotions motivate human beings more than anything else.[6] When emotions are unconscious they "have a higher biasing effect on decisions" and regardless, people "are unlikely to be fully aware of the unconscious influence their feelings are having on their decision making."[7] Emotions influence one's choice of action. They also influence how a person executes that action. "If a selected action, and its projected outcome, has strong emotional tags, then we are likely to act more decisively. If we have conflicting emotions, then we are more likely to be ambivalent about the proposed action."[8] Finally, "sadness biases preferences toward high-risk/high-reward options, whereas anxiety biases preference toward low-risk/low-reward options."[9]

Since emotions are an integral part of decision-making, whether it's an **Influencer's** decisions about power and influence or a **Target's** decision that matters to the **Influencer**, regulat-

---

[3]Sydney Finkelstein, Jo Whitehead, and Andrew Campbell. Think Again 64 (2008).

[4]Sydney Finkelstein, Jo Whitehead, and Andrew Campbell. Think Again 80 (2008).

[5]Sydney Finkelstein, Jo Whitehead, and Andrew Campbell. Think Again 81 (2008).

[6]G. Richard Shell and Mario Moussa. The Art of Woo 38 (2007).

[7]Sydney Finkelstein, Jo Whitehead, and Andrew Campbell. Think Again 45 (2008).

[8]Sydney Finkelstein, Jo Whitehead, and Andrew Campbell. Think Again 42 (2008).

[9]Rajagopal Raghunathan & Michel Tuan Pham. All Negative Moods are not Equal: Motivational Influences of Anxiety and Sadness on Decision Making, 79 Organizational Behavior and Human Decision Processes 56–77. http://www.columbia.edu/~tdp4/OBHDP1999A.pdf (last visited on November 19, 2010 (1999).

ing one's own emotions and influencing the emotions of others is important. Emotional intelligence is the ability to be aware of and regulate one's own and others' emotions to use one's emotions as **Influence Strategies** in one's thinking and actions.[10] "Emotions are contagious." "We influence each other's moods."[11] In doing so, we make it more or less likely that we will be successful in influencing them. Social intelligence "involves expressing ourselves in a way that produces a desired social result, like putting someone at ease. Artfully expressive people are viewed by others as confident and likeable and in general make favorable impressions."[12] These additional processes are further reason to develop a deep level of self-awareness about one's emotional reaction to power and influence.

As Wharton Management professor Sigal Barsade puts it, "people are walking mood inductors, continuously influencing the moods and then the judgments and behaviors of others."[13] Barsade ran an experiment in which a group of people simulated acting as managers who were meeting to allocate bonuses. Each person represented a single candidate and had two goals: (1) to get the best bonus for his or her candidate, and (2) to help the group allocate the bonus money in a way that would most benefit the company as a whole. Unbeknownst to the rest of the group, a trained actor, who was planted in the group, always spoke up first and made an identical argument. The only variable from group to group was the emotional tenor of that argument, which ranged from the positive: cheerful enthusiasm or serene warmth to the negative: hostile irritability or depressed sluggishness. When the actor used positive emotions, the groups allocated the bonus money more fairly and in ways to benefit the company as a whole.[14] There is evidence that subjects whose moods were more positive were more cooperative in making concessions. Evidence

---

[10]P. Salovey and J.D. Mayer. Emotional Intelligence 9 Imagination, Cognition and Personality 185–211, 189 (1990).

[11]Daniel Goleman. Working with Emotional Intelligence 164–65 (1998).

[12]Daniel Goleman. Social Intelligence 95 (2006).

[13]Sigal G. Barsade. The Ripple Effect: Emotional Contagion and its Influence on Group Behavior 47 Administrative Science Quarterly 644–675 http://links.jstor.org/sici?sici=0001-8392%28200212%2947%3A4%3C644%3ATREECA%3E2.0.CO%3B2-Z p. 25 (last visited March 2, 2010).

[14]Sigal G. Barsade. The Ripple Effect: Emotional Contagion and its Influence on Group Behavior 47 Administrative Science Quarterly 644–675 http://links.jstor.org/sici?sici=0001-8392%28200212%2947%3A4%3C644%3ATREECA%3E2.0.CO%3B2-Z p. 26 (last visited March 2, 2010).

also suggests that conflict can be escalated by negative moods.[15] What might that mean for you when negotiating on behalf of a client, or for your next raise? If your goal is to avoid or minimize conflict, what emotion-managing actions might you integrate into your **Influence Strategy** to make that happen?

Judge Jones is a great believer in the power of positive thinking and positive behavior, which he believes has enabled him to achieve in every endeavor. The science backs up his belief as being a highly effective **Influence Strategy**. In contrast, a lack of emotional and social intelligence can be fatal. Jack Griffin, who was ousted from the position of Time, Inc.'s CEO after less than six months, was described as "launch[ing] into tirades at meetings. He belittles people for not knowing or doing things he considers obvious. He calls people in for command-performance meetings at odd hours—seemingly just to remind them he can. He rarely says thanks."[16]

Without an awareness and self-regulation of one's emotions, a person is severely limited in his or her efforts to be influential. Engendering positive emotional responses in others is an important component of any **Influence Strategy**. Doing so begins with self-awareness of one's emotional state and is followed by self-regulation of emotions.

Regulating one's emotions starts with an awareness of when one is having an emotion. Noticing an emotion is followed by identifying the emotion. When you know what the emotions is, you can decide whether the time is appropriate for expressing it or whether it would be more strategic to put it aside. This is a skill that anyone can develop with practice.

Worksheet: Assessing Your Awareness and Self-Regulation of Emotions

Answer the following questions to assess your ability to regulate your emotions and their effects:

1. What is your process for recognizing and understanding your emotional state at any given moment? How effective are you?

2. What is your process for recognizing and understanding the emotional state of others at any given moment? How effective are you?

---

[15]Sigal G. Barsade. The Ripple Effect: Emotional Contagion and its Influence on Group Behavior 47 Administrative Science Quarterly 644–675 http://links.jstor.org/sici?sici=0001-8392%28200212%2947%3A4%3C644%3ATREECA%3E2.0.CO%3B2-Z p. 9 (last visited March 2, 2010).

[16]http://blogs.hbr.org/hbr/hbreditors/2011/02/jack__griffins__ouster__lessons__f.html (last looked February 21, 2011).

3. What is your process for regulating emotions in yourself? How effective are you?
4. What is your process for regulating emotions in others? How effective are you?

Interpreting Your Responses

If you aren't able to articulate the specific actions that you take to recognize, understand, and regulate your emotions and others', then you are in need of specific skill building through coaching and/or workshops.

Worksheet: Developing Your Emotional Awareness

1. How effective are you at identifying your emotions? If you have difficulty doing this, practice in the following ways:
   a. At any moment stop what you are doing and fill in the following sentence: Right now I feel . . .
   b. Explain the effect of your emotional state on your thinking and actions?
   c. Experience and then reflect on a highly charged situation. Do you cast it in terms of conclusions about the people or situation involved or the evidence of your feelings and everyone's visible behaviors? Ex. Which would you say: "Dave is being a jerk," or "I felt sad and angry when Dave said that I talk too much?" If the former, practice thinking in terms of the latter.
   d. Practice distinguishing between your thoughts and feelings? The statement, "I feel that he was wrong," is not an expression of a feeling.
2. Who do you hold responsible for your feelings? If you hold anyone other than yourself responsible, consider training or coaching to change this thinking.
3. Learn to consciously use your feelings to guide your decisions.
   a. Ask yourself how you will feel if you take or refrain from taking a particular action.
   b. Ask others who will be affected by your decision, how they will feel?
   c. Brainstorm or seek data on possible actions to improve your feelings or the feelings of others.
   d. Collect feedback data after you make a decision and act, analyze the data, and adjust your decision and actions based on the feelings generated after your decisions and actions.
4. How well do you listen and express empathy to others? How

are you measuring your listening and empathy skills? Strategic Communication workshops are ideal for developing these skills.

5. Learn to manage your negative feelings by doing the following:
   a. Acknowledge the feeling and experience it. Eventually all feelings subside.
   b. Be curious as to why you are having the feeling.
   c. Decide to move past the feeling and experiment with different approaches until you find one that is successful.

§ 3:15 Individuals and decision making: How can you influence the decision making of empowered individuals?—Hidden mindsets: Obstacles and opportunities

Individuals and groups use myriad, unspoken, and untested beliefs, assumptions, biases, and other hidden mindsets for interpreting and responding to a situation quickly and without conscious thought. That's exactly what happened to the farmer in Kansas and the storekeeper that reacted to Judge Jones as they did. Culture is defined by the shared and unspoken attitudes, beliefs, assumptions, and hidden biases that drive many of the decisions and actions within an organization. These hidden mindsets are "underlying frameworks" that unconsciously influence decision-making and "guide the way [people] reason and interpret the world."[1] Hidden mindsets present obstacles and opportunities.

They are obstacles when they cause an unfair action or one that actually decreases the effectiveness of the individual, group, or organization. They are often termed biases when triggered by an aspect of one's social identity like gender, race, religion, age, ethnicity, sexual orientation, or able-bodiness and are used unfairly to create an obstacle between a person and his or her goals. They engender equal frustration when triggered by a circumstance like socioeconomics, health, or family demands that that limit a person's opportunities. Hidden mindsets are opportunities when used by an **Influencer** to affect the thinking of his or her **Target** in a way that increases the likelihood that the **Target** will make a decision that is favorable to the **Influencer**.

[Section 3:15]

[1]Robert J. Marshak. Covert Processes at Work 11 (2006).

§ 3:16 Individuals and decision making: How can you influence the decision making of empowered individuals?—Hidden mindsets: Obstacles and opportunities—Biases and culture as obstacles

Unfair biases and culture create obstacles when they privilege a group of people, which is then able to acquire rewards and opportunities based on ascribed status rather than merit, over another group of people, whose interests are then subordinated to the higher-status group. This process seems to be a consequence of the fact that people appear to be programmed to use themselves "as an anchor or reference point"[1] when making decisions about other people. Thus, the majority social identity group in any system or organization creates the culture and biases by using themselves as the reference point in evaluating others' worthiness for rewards and opportunities. The experiment described in the following paragraph is a classic example of this decision-making phenomenon.

Participants in a study were asked to tap the rhythm of a popular song with their foot and then judge the likelihood that a listener, hearing only the tapping and knowing that it was a popular song, would be able to correctly identify the song. Tappers estimated that 50% of the listeners would guess correctly. Only 3% guessed correctly. The tappers estimated in the context of the rich data involved in hearing the song in their heads, while the listeners tried to identify the song with only the data of a rhythmic tapping and knowledge that it was a popular song.[2] The tappers couldn't help but use themselves as a reference point to predict the behavior of the listeners.

When this phenomenon is combined with the emotional nature of decisions explained earlier, it is not a leap to consider that the decisions about why the disparity occurred is the basis of stereotyping. If so few listeners were able to identify the song, which was so obvious to the tappers, it is not difficult to theorize that the tappers might decide that the listeners lacked competence instead of deciding that listeners had insufficient data to carry out their task with proficiency while the tappers were

---

[Section 3:16]

[1]Justin Kruger, Nicholas Epley, Jason Parker and Zhi-Wen Ng. Egocentrism Over E-Mail: Can We Communicate as Well as We Think?, 89 Journal of Personality and Social Psychology 925–36, 925 (2005).

[2]Justin Kruger, Nicholas Epley, Jason Parker and Zhi-Wen Ng. Egocentrism Over E-Mail: Can We Communicate as Well as We Think?, 89 Journal of Personality and Social Psychology 925–36, 925 (2005).

privileged with rich data. If the tappers were all of one social
identity while the listeners were all of another, a biased way of
making sense of the outcome would be to ascribe the differences
to the differences in social identity. When that happens, it is
termed implicit or unconscious bias, the unconscious tendency to
form associations between particular social identity groups and
attitudes, memories, and stereotypes. The implicit bias in gender
stereotyping is fairly well researched and has explained that the
associations that define gender stereotypes "emerge early in life,
often influencing children as young as three years old."[3] Their
influence is strong enough to create false memories of their
existence.[4] The bias in stereotyping can create significant
obstacles. The implicit biases arising from the stereotyping based
on any other social identity characteristic creates additional
obstacles. This book uses gender stereotyping as the example
because there is recent research on that particular topic as it
pertains to lawyers.

A recent study showed that "a diverse group of both male and
female law students implicitly associated judges with men . . .
and women with home and family . . . the more strongly male
participants associated judges with men . . . the more they
preferred that appellate judges possess masculine (as compared
to feminine) characteristics."[5] Further gender stereotyping affects
women in the legal profession. Stereotypes linking women to a
family caretaker role affect their prospects for career
advancement. Stereotypes about women's work styles, character
traits, and competencies interfere with their ability to advance to
the highest leadership positions. Women in roles that are
perceived to be male roles are judged more harshly than their
male colleagues.[6]

Gender bias also causes men, who assume the communal
characteristics of the family care-taker responsibilities, to be
perceived unfairly if their families are financially dependent. The

---

[3]Justin D. Levinson & Daniellle Young. Implicit Gender Bias in the Legal
Profession: An Empirical Study, 18 Duke Journal of Gender Law & Policy 5
(2010).

[4]Justin D. Levinson & Daniellle Young. Implicit Gender Bias in the Legal
Profession: An Empirical Study, 18 Duke Journal of Gender Law & Policy 8
(2010).

[5]Justin D. Levinson & Daniellle Young. Implicit Gender Bias in the Legal
Profession: An Empirical Study, 18 Duke Journal of Gender Law & Policy 1
(2010).

[6]Justin D. Levinson & Daniellle Young. Implicit Gender Bias in the Legal
Profession: An Empirical Study, 18 Duke Journal of Gender Law & Policy 9
(2010).

implicit bias is that men are primarily responsible for a family's financial security. If the family is able to rely on other means of support, they are judged more positively.[7] "Thus, so long as men do not violate gender norms by being extremely low in masculinity, their communal characteristics may be especially valued."[8] That seems to the theme in a complaint filed in December 2010 by a male associate who was fired by Deckert, LLP four months after returning from a paternity and FMLA leave of absence. The complaint alleges, "he became the primary caretaker of his children and had to care for [mentally ill wife] assuming a traditionally 'female' role." In particular he claimed that the "firm culture equates masculinity with relegating caretaking to women and working long hours in the office" and by taking the entire time allotted for paternity leave and extending his leave into FMLA leave, unlike other men at the firm, he "did not conform to Deckert's firm culture for males."[9] Regardless of whether these allegations are proven at trial, they are creating an emerging story about law firm culture.

Implicit bias goes even deeper to create contextual standards for success that are biased against women. The culture measures career success against a model that privileges the person who is able to work without regard for the consequences on that person's personal life. Access to promotions, plum assignments, formal mentoring relationships, and resources and being more influential is reserved for the privileged person.[10] This model of career success is a consequence of research that measured the success of subjects who were men with stay-at-home wives. "When one group—in this case men—is the norm, the other group's behavior—in this case women—is seen as the deviant pattern that required explanation."[11]

The bias continues with the standards used to identify the behaviors of successful leaders in roles that are seen as stereotypi-

---

[7]J. M. Riggs. Mandates for Mothers and Fathers: Perceptions of Breadwinner and Care Givers. 37 Sex Roles 565–580 (1977).

[8]Amanda B. Diekman. Negotiating the Double Bind: Interpersonal and Instrumental Evaluations of Dominance. 56 Sex Roles 551–561 (2007).

[9]Ayanna v. Deckert (Complaint Introduction) http://pdfserver.amlaw.com/nlj/AyannavDechertsuit.pdf (last visited March 4, 2011).

[10]Mary Shapiro, Cynthia Ingols, and Stacy Blake-Beard. Confronting Career Double Binds:Implications for Women, Organizations, and Career Practitioners, 34 Journal of Career Development 309–333 (2008).

[11]Virginia Valian. Why So Slow? The Advancement of Women (1999).

cally male roles.[12] For example, gender stereotypes assign positive attributes to men who are dominant and independent
("agentic") and women are warm and kind ("communal").[13]
Individuals are judged more positively if their behaviors are
congruent with stereotypes for each of their social roles. They are
also judged more positively if their behaviors are congruent with
their professional roles. Agentic behavior is expected and valued
in certain roles and communal behavior in others.[14] Dominance,
standing up under pressure and being aggressive "was particularly valued in the business-competition condition[15] and [warmth]
in the caretaking condition."[16] Agentic female applicants for a job
considered to require more communal skills are evaluated as
equally competent as agentic male applicants, but less socially
skilled and desirable to hire.[17] This is similar to a 1998 finding
that traditional women were more likeable than feminists but
less respected.[18] It becomes complicated for lawyers. The role of
an advocate in court or as a negotiator is different from the role
in client relationship development and management or leadership of colleagues and staff.

Further, the ideal levels of dominance appear to be higher for a
man than a woman; women may be evaluated negatively, less desirable to hire, and less attractive for being too dominant and
self-promoting.[19] Many of the successful women lawyers who were
interviewed, and who are of the Boomer Generation, seem to

---

[12]Amanda B. Diekman. Negotiating the Double Bind: Interpersonal and
Instrumental Evaluations of Dominance. 56 Sex Roles 551–561, 552 (2007).

[13]T. Eckes and H.M. Trautner. The Developmental Social Psychology of
Gender 123–174 (2000).

[14]Amanda B. Diekman. Negotiating the Double Bind: Interpersonal and
Instrumental Evaluations of Dominance. 56 Sex Roles 551–561, 558 (2007).

[15]M. A. Cejka and A. H. Eagly. Gender-Stereotypic Images of Occupations
Correspond to the Sex Segregation of Employment, 25 Personality and Social
Psychology Bulletin, 413–423 (1999).

[16]Amanda B. Diekman. Negotiating the Double Bind: Interpersonal and
Instrumental Evaluations of Dominance. 56 Sex Roles 551–561, 560 (2007).

[17]L. A. Rudman and P. Glick. Feminized Management and Backlash
Toward Agentic Women: The hidden Costs to Women of a Kinder, Gentler
Image of Middle Managers, 77 Journal of Personality and Social Psychology
1004–1010 (1999).

[18]T. K. MacDonald and M. P. Zanna, Cross-Dimensional Ambivalence
Toward Social Groups: Can Ambivalence Affect Intentions to Hire Feminists?,
24 Personality and Social Psychology Bulletin 427–441(1998).

[19]A. H. Eagly, M. G. Makhijani, and B. G. Klonsky. Gender and the Evaluation of Leaders: A Meta-Analysis, 111 Psychological Bulletin 3–22 (1992); L. A.
Rudman Self-Promotion as a Risk Factor for Women: The Costs and Benefits of

have effectively navigated this narrow line. They were adjudged dominant enough, but not too dominant, in the eyes of those they needed to influence. Women in all-male task groups were judged to be more influential when they acted in a friendly, supportive manner, which emphasized cooperation.[20] Women who spoke without hesitation and with a neutral facial expression were perceived as less influential than men who were judged to behave similarly, but this difference disappeared when a friendlier facial expression and more forward-leaning was added.[21] Buffering dominance with warmth, regardless of gender, increases the likelihood that a person will be more favorably evaluated for interpersonal skills.[22]

There is a tendency to evaluate men more favorably than women on competence and satisfaction with leadership, but not on perceptions of leadership styles,[23] yet autocratic and other "masculine" styles of leadership are judged more favorably when exhibited by men. The styles that favor women are friendly, cooperative, and interpersonally-oriented. These behaviors enhance women's but not men's status and ability to influence a group.[24]

Interestingly there are no gender differences for lawyers in evaluating the characteristics of an effective negotiator. On the contrary "men and women are similar in approach and effectiveness when working on behalf of clients."[25] It is difficult to say whether the result is a consequence of the role of negotiator/ lawyer trumping the role of being a woman because of a higher perceived status, because negotiating/advocating on behalf of a client is perceived to be stereotypic communal behavior, or

---

Countersterotypical Impression Management, 74 Journal of Personality and Social Psychology 629–645 (1998).

[20]C. L. Ridgeway. Status in Groups: The Importance of Motivation, 47 American Sociological Review 76–88 (1982).

[21]L.L. Carli, S.J.LaFleur, and C.C. Loeber. Nonverbal Behavior, Gender, and Influence, 68 Journal of Personality and Social Psychology 1030–1042 (1995).

[22]Amanda B. Diekman. Negotiating the Double Bind: Interpersonal and Instrumental Evaluations of Dominance. 56 Sex Roles 551–561, 558 (2007).

[23]A. H. Eagly, M. G. Makhijani, and B. G. Klonsky. Gender and the Evaluation of Leaders: A Meta-Analysis, 111 Psychological Bulletin 3–22, 12 (1992).

[24]A. H. Eagly, M. G. Makhijani, and B. G. Klonsky. Gender and the Evaluation of Leaders: A Meta-Analysis, 111 Psychological Bulletin 3–22, 12 (1992).

[25]A.K. Schneider, C.H. Tinsely, S. Cheldelin, and E. T. Amanatullah. Likeability v. Competence: The Impossible Choice Faced by Female Politicians, Attenuated by Lawyers, 17 Duke J. Gender L. & Policy 363, 373, 375 (2010).

because television has made the role of the female lawyer more acceptable and familiar.[26]

If anything, there is ambiguity. It is difficult to know with any degree of certainty which behaviors will work to create the conditions for a merit- or logic-based evaluation of one's actions rather than one driven by a hidden bias or culture. Ambiguity creates a level of risk. This brings us to an interesting observation from appellate lawyer, Mary-Christine ("M.C.") Sungaila. M.C., who recently filed a brief in the United States Supreme Court, on behalf of Wal-Mart, and who has successfully briefed and argued a broad range of appeals in California as well as nationally and internationally on behalf of Fortune 500 companies and leading human rights organizations, like Amnesty International. A win in the Inter-American Court of Human Rights was described as "one of the most important legal victories for international women's rights in decades." She has been named one of the Top 100 Women Litigators in California by the Daily Journal and received the Alpha Phi International Fraternity Alumni award for career achievement. Her expert commentary has appeared in a variety of publications ranging from the ABA Journal and National Law Journal to the Los Angeles Times and USA Today.[27] M.C. knows something about taking risks.

M.C. believes that "until women themselves take risks on their own behalf and on behalf of other women" it is unlikely that women will achieve power in law firms "on a widespread basis." She recounted a story shared with her by guests at a dinner party. A wife was offered a position and a salary, both of which she was ecstatic to have received. Her husband asked her about negotiating for more, which she hadn't considered doing, because she was afraid that the offer would be withdrawn. He encouraged his wife to negotiate and told her specifically how to do it. In contrast, when he had been offered a position, he pulled out the organization chart and responded that he wanted a different position, which had budgetary control and would be better for his career. His response worked to his advantage.

M.C.'s story shows two starkly different ways of thinking about opportunities and the consequences of risk-taking. The consequences of any risks women take on their own behalf and on behalf of others are not clear enough that attempting to avoid

---

[26]A.K. Schneider, C.H. Tinsely, S. Cheldelin, and E. T. Amanatullah. Likeability v. Competence: The Impossible Choice Faced by Female Politicians, Attenuated by Lawyers, 17 Duke J. Gender L. & Policy 363, 378–380 (2010).

[27]http://www.swlaw.com/attorneys/mc_sungaila (last visited March 9, 2011).

them, as a default response, is justified. Indeed, the only thing
that is clear is that routinely attempting to avoid these risks
leaves opportunities behind. At a minimum, there is an opportunity to experiment intelligently now and learn how to be
more influential later.

"The research on advocacy suggests that one way women might
align the core feminine stereotype with assertive bargaining
would be to reframe negotiations for raises or promotions as
other-oriented (e.g., for the communal welfare of her client, work
team, or law firm) rather than self-interested."[28] Use statements
that emphasize the connection between the outcome requested
and the goal of setting a positive precedent for a larger group or
the organization itself.[29] Some researchers suggest that if a
woman doesn't behave femininely enough, i.e., empathetic and
sensitive, she will face a backlash when she aggressively
advocates. One study showed that when men and women flirt in
negotiations, they are "perceived as more likeable."[30]

There is no question that system-wide changes in perceptions
and decision making are needed. That's the purpose of every diversity and inclusion initiative. Attempts to change the system
must include initiating conversations among higher and lower
privileged groups about the complexity of identity, the hidden
biases that we all unconsciously use because of our unique life
experiences, and the risks of making bad decisions because of an
unwillingness or inability to surface and discuss these hidden
biases. Perhaps the most important strategy is to nurture
sponsorship relationships and expand one's prominence in powerful networks.[31] Sylvia Hewlett reported on a study about the effect of having a sponsor. A sponsor or champion is a person of a
higher-privileged status who advocates on behalf of another, who
is of a lower privileged status. The privilege is often related to
years of experience. Privilege is also a consequence of the difference in social identities with the majority identity in any system

---

[28]A.K. Schneider, C.H. Tinsely, S. Cheldelin, and E. T. Amanatullah.
Likeability v. Competence: The Impossible Choice Faced by Female Politicians,
Attenuated by Lawyers, 17 Duke J. Gender L. & Policy 363, 381 (2010).

[29]A.K. Schneider, C.H. Tinsely, S. Cheldelin, and E. T. Amanatullah.
Likeability v. Competence: The Impossible Choice Faced by Female Politicians,
Attenuated by Lawyers, 17 Duke J. Gender L. & Policy 363, 382 (2010).

[30]A.K. Schneider, C.H. Tinsely, S. Cheldelin, and E. T. Amanatullah.
Likeability v. Competence: The Impossible Choice Faced by Female Politicians,
Attenuated by Lawyers, 17 Duke J. Gender L. & Policy 363, 383 (2010).

[31]A.K. Schneider, C.H. Tinsely, S. Cheldelin, and E. T. Amanatullah.
Likeability v. Competence: The Impossible Choice Faced by Female Politicians,
Attenuated by Lawyers, 17 Duke J. Gender L. & Policy 363, 384 (2010).

constituting the privileged group. The advocacy occurs in the nature of advancing someone for a promotion, raise, work assignment, or any other important career opportunity.

> What's been holding women back, the study found, isn't a male conspiracy but rather a surprising absence of advocacy from men and women in positions of power. Women who are qualified to lead simply don't have the powerful backing necessary to inspire, propel, and protect themselves on their journey through upper management. Women lack, in a word, *sponsorship*.[32]

JoAnne Epps credits her predecessor for making sure that she had the experiences that would position her for the role of dean of the law school when he retired. When Judge Jones went through the vetting process before appointment to the Federal Bench, "everyone was a sponsor in that they all had great things to say about [his] appointment." According to Ritva Sotamaa, successful in-house lawyers typically have champions from both the legal and business side of the organization. This type of "double support" is often key to how successful you are perceived to be in your job and what kind of career opportunities you are offered later on.

Gender differences appear when a woman acts on her own behalf, making it more important that female lawyers and lawyers in minority social identity groups have a sponsor and special strategies when negotiating on their own behalf. If so, consider the following: (1) highlight your status and role; (2) use your training as a lawyer; (3) emphasize that your request will benefit a team or organization (to align your action with the expected, communal stereotypes held about women); (4) fight against stereotyping through efforts to change the entire system; and (5) nurture sponsorship relationships.

§ 3:17 Individuals and decision making: How can you influence the decision making of empowered individuals?—Hidden mindsets: Obstacles and opportunities—Hidden beliefs, values, assumptions, and culture as opportunities

People often reach particular decisions because of the directive effect of subtle, imperceptible primes. A prime can be anything that effectively directs a **Target's** thinking and behavior. Experiment with the following and see what happens. Give a person a

---

[32]Sylvia Ann Hewlett. The Real Benefit of Finding a Sponsor. Harvard Business Review http://blogs.hbr.org/hbr/hewlett/2011/01/the__real__benefit__o f__finding__a.html (last visited January 28, 2011).

piece of paper with "pen" on it and say, "I am giving you this pen and paper. Write down as many words possible in 30 seconds." Are the words pen or paper on the list? Try the experiments: Mention the idea of going to the library to people and see if they lower their voices. Rub your face or shake a foot and see how many people mimic you. Use words like "adhere," "agree," or "comply" and see whether you can get someone to conform to your opinion or idea. Research experiments have shown that triggers of those types affected the behavior of the subjects who were exposed to the behavior.[1] Robert Cialdini identified six factors that prime specific behavior. The first is reciprocation or repaying someone in kind.

§3:18 Individuals and decision making: How can you influence the decision making of empowered individuals?—Hidden mindsets: Obstacles and opportunities—Reciprocation

On an unconscious level, people are driven "to repay, in kind, what another person has provided us."[1] If you know what "repay" and "in kind" means to your **Target**, this can be an effective influence lever. However, one's awareness of the reciprocation process may diffuse its intended impact. Taking a prospective client to lunch is not enough to influence the **Target** to give you business and may not even lead to a second lunch.

People seem to confuse the norm of reciprocation and taking someone to lunch with building deep relationships, which create deep and mutual value for the parties. Reneé Bergman explains the foolishness in thinking that you can meet someone once, take the person to lunch, and then when the person needs legal work, he or she will call you. She emphasizes the need to develop relationships over time because people work with people that they like and trust. Trust develops over time with the sharing of interests and stories about each other's personal lives.

Reciprocation seems to be used frequently in social media marketing with apparent expectations that if we follow someone on Twitter that person will follow us too, if we retweet someone

---

[Section 3:17]

[1]Jessica M. Nolan, P. Wesley Schultz, Robert B. Cialdini, Noah J. Goldstein, and Vladas Griskevicius. Normative Social Influence is Underdetected, 34 Personality and Social Psychology Bulletin 913, 914 (2008).

[Section 3:18]

[1]Robert B. Cialdini, Ph.D. Influence The Psychology of Persuasion. 17 (1993).

that person will retweet us, and if we share the business news of someone with our LinkedIn contacts he or she will do the same for us in the future. These expectations are not always met. Social media connections are not a substitute for developing deep relationships, but they may set the stage for a relationship that deepens over time. The deepening may occur virtually and may eventually lead to a face-to-face meeting.

§ 3:19   Individuals and decision making: How can you influence the decision making of empowered individuals?—Hidden mindsets: Obstacles and opportunities—Acting consistent with prior commitment

People are somewhat motivated to behave in ways that appear to be consistent with prior statements and actions. If they promise to do something in the future, they may feel constrained to act consistently with that promise.[1] Further, this behavior is one cornerstone to developing trust. Not following through on one's promises certainly undermines trust. Part of one's attempts to influence anyone should include building a foundation of trust.

Sometimes the need to continue consistent behavior causes an unfortunate and wasteful result. Failed information technology projects that seem to take on a life of their own before finally being discarded exemplify the apparent effect of "an escalating commitment to a failing course of action"[2] where people have committed substantial resources to the project and they are not aware of an alternative course of action.[3] This is a risk that is likely familiar to any **Influencer** who has committed substantial time and psychological energy in attempts to develop business from a particular **Target**, who is unable or unwilling to drive business in the **Influencer's** direction. If the **Target's** behavior seems the least bit ambiguous, it's easy to believe that business will flow in the **Influencer's** direction in the future, especially if the **Influ-**

[Section 3:19]

[1]Robert B. Cialdini, Ph.D. Influence The Psychology of Persuasion. 57, 67 (1993).

[2]Mark Keil, Richard Mixon, Timo Saarinen, and Virpi Tuunainen. Understanding Runaway Information Technology Projects: Results from an International Research Program Based on Escalation Theory, 11 Journal of Management Information Systems 65–85, 65 (1995).

[3]Mark Keil, Richard Mixon, Timo Saarinen, and Virpi Tuunainen Understanding Runaway Information Technology Projects: Results from an International Research Program Based on Escalation Theory, 11 Journal of Management Information Systems 65–85, 73 (1995).

encer and **Target** enjoy each other's company. Asking the direct question may be necessary to find out whether the **Target** will drive business in your direction. However, despite the answer to that question, if business doesn't flow within a reasonable period of time and the relationship feels unbalanced, it may be best to walk away and find another, more appropriate **Target**. Walking away may feel like a loss which, as explained earlier, may make the transition a greater challenge. Remember, time is a precious and limited resource and it is not a loss if the relationship is unbalanced.

§ 3:20   Individuals and decision making: How can you influence the decision making of empowered individuals?—Hidden mindsets: Obstacles and opportunities—Social proof

Social proof is a consequence of feeling part of a group and being influenced by the actions of group members, regardless of the logic of and reasons for engaging in a particular behavior. It is an extremely powerful prime.[1] Additionally, people tend to deny that social proof has affected their decision-making. For example, the presence of a crowd will make it statistically less likely that any single person will render help to someone in need. Yet, when asked, individuals will generally deny the impact of the crowd's actions on their decision not to render help. In an experiment in which individuals in a group were asked to estimate the distance a beam of light had moved under conditions that made it impossible to execute this task with any accuracy, the subsequent speakers' estimates were correlated to the answer of the earlier speakers at statistically significant levels. Group members denied that their estimates were influenced by the answers of others in the group who had spoken first. The need to interpret our own actions as rational and under our control leads us to deny evidence that they are not, making social proof an extremely powerful prime.

> Individuals place greater weight on introspective thoughts and beliefs related to their decision to conform than to the behavioral evidence of their conformity. For example, if Jane is told that most students at her university support a change in the early decision policy, then she is more likely to support the change in policy herself, compared to those who are told that most students do not

---

[Section 3:20]

[1]Robert B. Cialdini, Ph.D. Influence The Psychology of Persuasion. 116 (1993).

support the change. However, when asked why she supports the change in policy, Jane is likely to cite personal thoughts and reasoning as the most influential cause for her support.[2]

Social proof, if available to you, will be a powerful part of your **Influence Strategy**, but it requires proof that other people are already doing what you want your **Target** to do. Social proof is closely related to one's reputation, i.e., that a large number of people hold a particular belief about a person. If you have given a seminar that was well-attended and well-liked and the attendees tell their friends, then the next time you give that seminar, don't be surprised if the audience is larger. If you have a reputation as the person in your organization to go to for the answer, don't be surprised if more and more people seek you out for your knowledge. People tend to do what others in their group are doing.

Social proof assumes the existence of a network of people who like you or what you do. More often than not, lawyers will say that most of their business comes from existing clients or referrals from existing clients. That's social proof in action with relationship building as a critical skill to its development and use. That segues nicely into the next section.

§ 3:21   Individuals and decision making: How can you influence the decision making of empowered individuals?—Hidden mindsets: Obstacles and opportunities—Likeability

People are more likely to comply with requests from people that they like, want to be near, or want to be like.[1] Likeability is subjective although people tend to like those, who they decide are physically attractive[2] or share similar opinions, personality traits, background, life-style, physical dress and style, interests, or social identity characteristics. Likeability also results from the appearance of confidence from a particular body posture, mood, and

---

[2]Jessica M. Nolan, P. Wesley Schultz, Robert B. Cialdini, Noah J. Goldstein and Vladas Griskevicius. Normative Social Influence is Underdetected, 34 Personality and Social Psychology Bulletin 913, 914 (2008).

[Section 3:21]

[1]Robert B. Cialdini, Ph.D. Influence The Psychology of Persuasion. 167 (1993).

[2]Robert B. Cialdini, Ph.D. Influence The Psychology of Persuasion. 171 (1993).

verbal style.[3] People also tend to like others who offer a compliment even if they know the substance is false.[4]

There is a tremendous amount of ambiguity in determining likeability. This means that, at the very least, anyone who wants to develop effectiveness in influencing others must consider what he or she can do to make himself or herself more likeable. This demands a consciousness of how one dresses, uses voice and body, shares the details of one's identity with others. Jane Dalton considered her northern Ohio accent to be "a bit of a disadvantage," that she worked to "overcome with content and tone." Experiment with the myriad variables that affect likeability and try to determine what you can do to increase your likeability.

The behaviors associated with likeability seem to vary depending on the role of the **Influencer**, the particular predisposition of the **Target**, and the context of the interaction. The Referent **Power Base** discussed in § 4:2 is a consequence of being likable. If you superimpose the effect of social proof, likeability breeds more likeability.

§ 3:22 Individuals and decision making: How can you influence the decision making of empowered individuals?—Hidden mindsets: Obstacles and opportunities—Authority

The relative differences in positions of authority, because of formal position, may influence a person in the lower position to defer to the will of the person in the higher position.[1] This phenomenon results from the assumed ability to mete out rewards, resources, or punishments. Symbols of authority include titles, clothing, jewelry, automobiles, or other toys.[2] However, there are limits to the power of authority. A person may agree to abide by the will of a person in a formal position of power, like a CEO, because he or she is obligated to do so, while looking for ways to circumvent the authority through the use of informal power and networks.

------

[3]Robert B. Cialdini, Ph.D. Influence The Psychology of Persuasion. 173–74 (1993).

[4]Robert B. Cialdini, Ph.D. Influence The Psychology of Persuasion. 174–75 (1993).

[Section 3:22]

[1]Robert B. Cialdini, Ph.D. Influence The Psychology of Persuasion. 226 (1993).

[2]Robert B. Cialdini, Ph.D. Influence The Psychology of Persuasion. 222–229 (1993).

§ 3:23 Individuals and decision making: How can you influence the decision making of empowered individuals?—Hidden mindsets: Obstacles and opportunities—Scarcity

People tend to want that which they think is rare. A related phenomenon is that people are more motivated to avoid a loss than they are by the thought of gaining something.[1] Loss avoidance was discussed in Chapter 1 in the context of an **Influencer's** efforts to change the way he or she thinks about using power and influence. The fear of losing anything is enough to create inertia, as explained in the business development example. If you want to influence someone not to make a change, reminding her or him of a potential loss might be sufficient. An **Influencer** should try to identify the things that the **Target** values and would not want to lose, including those aspects of a relationship with the **Influencer** or the **Target's** relationships with clients, customers, vendors, colleagues, or employees.

Scarcity priming is one reason that lawyers with expertise that is scarce experience relative price insensitivity for their services in the marketplace, while even the best lawyers, who practice in fields where there are many talented lawyers, feel a downward pricing pressure. Dara Green focuses her practice on foreign tax planning. She is a lawyer at Baker & McKenzie, LLP, a leading firm for foreign tax law advice. This field of law has relatively few lawyers in it. Dara shares the following lesson that she has learned:

> If you are in a specialty field, you can rise above everyone else. One of the best things you can do for yourself is to find something that interests you and that other people don't know as well as you do. Become the expert on the issue and then speak about it. This will help you develop a reputation as an expert in a niche field. The more you speak about the topic, the more questions you will be asked. New questions will lead you to learn more about the topic and deepen your expertise and reputation as an expert. Your deeper expertise will lead to more requests for you to talk on the topic.

There is another aspect to scarcity priming that creates obstacles in planning for success and taking steps toward one's goals. Thinking that critical resources necessary to one's success and happiness are limited is often followed by feelings of anxiety, sadness, or being enervated. Thinking and feeling like that

---

[Section 3:23]

[1]Robert B. Cialdini, Ph.D. Influence The Psychology of Persuasion. 238 (1993).

impairs the ability to notice opportunities and also to make the best decisions. For instance, when a person believes that there aren't enough clients or work, he or she might try to cling to a relationship that is unfruitful, believing that's the only possibility for developing business. Consequently, he or she might not try to find and develop new relationships with potential clients and referral sources or notice the other potential clients and business.

§ 3:24 Individuals and decision making: How can you influence the decision making of empowered individuals?—Hidden mindsets: Obstacles and opportunities—Culture

The culture of any system, organization, or group is a hugely powerful and invisible prime. The culture at Jones Day is cultivated by leadership and communicated internally and externally and is one of the best examples of this priming power.

Jones Day partners do not complain about the lack of transparency in the compensation decision-making process, while in other firms' transparency in this process is expected and discussed before a person will accept an offer of partnership. How can a law firm's culture quench the craving of some of the top lawyers in the world for evidence of how their compensation was determined? Lawyers, by nature, crave evidence, and one would think that lawyers especially would want to be able to decide if the decisions about their compensation were fair. The culture creates beliefs among partners at Jones Day that the compensation process fairly values lawyers' respective contributions to the firm, and allowing a small group of trusted people to make compensation decisions in secret is valuable for the entire firm.

Partner Carrie Hogan explains that lawyers at Jones Day are happy and feel no incentive to horde work for themselves. If a lawyer brings in a client or matter for the firm, he or she is going to staff it with the best people rather than think about which part of a client billing they will get credit for. "Partners are paid based on their contributions, leadership, collegiality and reputation, and not on client originations. . . . Hours are considered, but there's no formula."[1] The firm has a single managing partner, who was appointed without vote by the prior managing partner. He makes all compensation decisions and leadership appointments with information and advice presented by an 11-member

---

[Section 3:24]

[1]Amanda Royal. Jones Day Keeps its Paychecks Private. http://www.law.com/jsp/article.jsp?id=1202465019083 (last visited November 11, 2010).

advisory committee, proposed by the Managing Partner and voted on by the partners. This past year, they had a record number of women appointed to the committee.

According to Carrie, the system is not about being a power broker. On the contrary, Carrie explains that the more work her clients send her way, the more lawyers her clients will need, and the more money there will be for the firm at the end of the year. Carrie's decision to stay at the firm, despite controlling a significant enough book of business to be a Wanderer if she wanted, is a matter of feeling that she and the firm are a good fit. She is not forced to do administrative work yet is given the decision-making power inherent in being the head of the Product Liability Practice in Chicago. She enjoys the autonomy to do interesting and challenging work, surrounded by people she really likes, and with the freedom to be a "creative dresser." She likes that they "let me be the individual lawyer that I am." This is a statement about her identity and fit within the culture of the firm. The power of this context is so influential that outsiders often put it this way: "the Kool-Aid must taste good."[2]

If you visit the Jones Day Web site and search the site for the word "culture," you come up with 200 hits. Compare competitors' sites and you will see how unusual this is. Here are a few examples of the different Jones Day Web pages talking about culture:

- Our structure fosters a *culture* of teamwork and discourages competition among offices and lawyers;
- We recognize that Partners and associates alike contribute to the Firm in a variety of ways, and our lawyers are compensated according to their overall contributions. At the same time, our lawyers honor a *culture* of discretion about matters related to compensation; unlike other firms, we do not publish each lawyer's billable hours and compensation for the entire Firm to see; and
- A *culture* of respect.

---

[2]Amanda Royal. Jones Day Keeps its Paychecks Private. http://www.law.com/jsp/article.jsp?id=1202465019083 (last visited November 11, 2010).

§ 3:25 Individuals and decision making: How can you influence the decision making of empowered individuals?—Unconscious blockers

Unexpressed emotions, such as anger, sadness, or fear, can block one's ability to be influential.[1] When anxiety is present, a person will do anything to reduce it. If you ask a person or group to make a significant change, which is often perceived as a loss, you may trigger an anxiety reaction. If you behave in a way that triggers an unconscious memory of a prior, unpleasant relationship dynamic for someone, you may inadvertently trigger that person's defense mechanisms. The more you know about the people you want to influence, the more successful you can be. Rather than focusing efforts on trying to avoid the triggering of anxiety responses and defense mechanisms, which is nearly impossible, it is more productive to focus on how to recognize and reduce the responses when they happen to you or to someone you are trying to influence. Ritva Sotamaa has learned that "every person has issues, preferences, and attitudes, and some people even have historical baggage that impacts how they think about things. Typically, you learn about such things only after a while of working together."

Following are two examples from my coaching and consulting practices. The first arises from an individual coaching consultation and the latter from a group processes consultation.

Several years ago, I was coaching Jason, the director of the professional administrative support staff in a large law firm with multiple offices in the U.S. During the course the coaching engagement, Jason had repeatedly stated that he wanted more encouragement, praise, and direction from David (his boss). At one session, when I asked Jason about this stated desire, Jason acknowledged that David would tell him if he were not doing a good job and said, "I know that Dad will tell me if I'm not doing well."

My goal was to get Jason to realize that he was looking at his interaction with David as if the pair were father and son and then distinguish his relationship with David. Had I confronted Jason with a logical argument and told him my conclusion, that I thought his desire for lavish praise from David was unreasonable and he should stop, I probably would have triggered unhelpful emotions and defensiveness. Instead, I listened empathetically

---

[Section 3:25]

[1]Robert J. Marshak. Covert Processes in the Workplace. 10 (2006).

and then used feedback, which essentially repeated back to Jason what I had heard him say and accentuating the word "Dad." This sufficed to reach the first part of my goal for Jason, which was for Jason to realize what was motivating his need for approval from David. Sometimes the best **Influence Strategy** is to listen with empathy and share classic feedback of what you heard.

The second example arose in a process consultation for a group of six equity partners. The managing partner, 56-year-old Alex, and the partner in charge of the tax department, 41-year-old Pat, weren't talking to each other. Several weeks earlier Pat had wanted to fire a paralegal in Pat's department. In a screaming incident, the paralegal had made a detailed threat to kill Pat, which led Alex, Pat, and others to wonder about the paralegal's emotional stability, but not enough to take immediate action. Pat's decision to fire the paralegal came several weeks after the screaming incident. When Pat told Alex about Pat's decision, Alex told Pat that Alex was concerned that an immediate firing might trigger the paralegal to carry out the threat and put Pat in danger. Alex directed Pat to wait until the paralegal received the annual review in a few weeks, which would probably cause the paralegal to quit. Pat became furious with Alex. Pat's anger triggered feelings of frustration in Alex. Communication between them broke down completely.

Upon further discussion, it emerged that Alex wanted to protect Pat from making a bad decision and Pat wanted the power to make firing decisions in Pat's department without interference from Alex, especially when Pat perceived that the decision would eliminate a personal danger. Alex and Pat shared a goal of how best to protect Pat but differed on the best process. They also disagreed about who should have the right to make the decisions that affected Pat's life. The implicit questions are: Who has the role and decision-making power to hire and fire people within Pat's department? Who has the power to decide how best to protect Pat? These are questions about identity and the dynamic between Alex and Pat including behaviors that one might expect to see in a parent-child relationship. How might Alex or Pat have handled the situation differently to avoid a break down in communication? How might each have successfully influenced the other? How might they have negotiated a result that neither had considered?

Worksheet: Influencing the Decision Making of Empowered Individuals

Fill in the following chart:

Effective Influencers

Decision-Making Motivator or Blocker	When it is effective?	When is it ineffective?	Give an example of how you would use it

§ 3:26 Chapter summary

- Determine where in a system, organization, or group the power, relative to the decisions that matter to you, exists using existing documents and the data your collect from questions and personal observation about how people behave toward one another.
- All organizations are political. Political dynamics may be autocratic, bureaucratic, technocratic, in a codetermination design, a representative democracy design, or a direct de-

mocracy design. Be aware of the dynamics and how they can be influenced differently.

- The decision-making processes of empowered individuals are susceptible to various types of influence, which may motivate or block a particular decision. They include logic and reason, interests, aspirations and inspirations, emotions, hidden mindsets, and unconscious blockers. Lawyers may rely too heavily on logic and reason. Effective **Influence Strategies** will use multiple avenues to affect the decision-making targets.

Chapter 4

Personal Power Bases

> **KeyCite®:** Cases and other legal materials listed in KeyCite Scope can be researched through the KeyCite service on Westlaw®. Use KeyCite to check citations for form, parallel references, prior and later history, and comprehensive citator information, including citations to other decisions and secondary materials.

§ 4:1   Chapter focus and questions

Power Bases are personal sources of unique energy for an **Influencer** to use to affect the decision making of his or her **Target.** This chapter explains five different **Power Bases**, options for developing or expanding them, and how to use them in an **Influence Strategy.**

Questions to Consider:

1. What are the five different **Power Bases?** Give different examples for each.
2. How are **Power Bases** used in **Influence Strategies**?
3. Where are your strongest sources of power? Where are your weakest? What can you do to develop or expand your **Power Bases**?

§ 4:2   The Power Bases

Power is a person's potential to affect "a change in the belief, attitude, or behavior of a person (the target of influence), which results from the action of another person (an influencing agent)."[1] It has been suggested that all "power is the capacity to influence another person or group to accept one's own ideas or plans."[2] An empowered and expansive view is that an **Influencer's** capacity is both personally held and a result of the **Influencer's** networks. There are five **Power Bases** explained in this chapter: (1) Control over Resources; (2) Formal Position; (3) Referent; (4) Expert; and (5) Network Position. The first four are within the direct control of the **Influencer**. The first four **Power Bases** are one's own personal powers. The last, Network Position power, is the power of others available because of one's relationships.

Control over Resources is a **Power Base** arising from the ability to incentivize behavior with the promise of a reward or coerce behavior with the threat of a penalty. The reward is bestowing a resource on the **Target**. A positive incentive is anything that the **Target** desires from a bonus, knowledge, or special privilege. A penalty is anything that the **Target** wants to avoid, like an undesirable work assignment or termination. In essence, if the **Target** complies and engages in the desired behavior he or she will receive a benefit and if not he or she will receive a penalty.

[Section 4:2]

[1]Bert H. Raven. The Bases of Power and the Power/Interaction Model of Interpersonal Influence. 8 Analysis of Social Issues & Public Policy 1-22, 1 (2008).

[2]Larry E. Greiner and Virginia E. Schein. Power and Organization Development. 13 (1988).

Thinking about a positive or negative consequence influences the **Target's** decision-making and behavior.

Formal Position is a **Power Base** that arises "from social norms requiring that the target of influence comply with the request or order of the influencing agent."[3] The **Target** believes that he or she must decide and act consistently with the **Influencer's** wants, needs, and expectations because of the **Influencer's** higher position than the **Target** in a system, organization, or group, regardless of whether the **Influencer** was voted in or appointed to the higher position. Formal Position also creates a **Power Base** in the lower positioned person if it imposes a feeling of responsibility on the higher positioned person to someone who is fully dependent on him or her.[4] One might term that the power of guilt.

Referent power stems from a **Target's** desire to be similar to, liked by, or near the **Influencer**. Powers overlap so that "personal approval from someone whom we like can result in quite powerful reward power; and a threat of rejection or disapproval from someone we value highly can serve as a source of powerful coercive power."[5] Referent power is also in the power of reciprocity "if someone does something beneficial for us, then we should feel an obligation to reciprocate."[6] In the previous chapter we looked at the mercurial nature of reciprocity. Referent power is also in the nature of equity if a person thinks he or she has harmed someone and owes a debt to bring the relationship back to an even keel.[7]

Expert power is the power existing because one holds rare information and expertise that is in high demand. It flows from having a high level of knowledge or experience that others depend on. It is like a resource that will influence others to make deci-

---

[3]Bert H. Raven. The Bases of Power and the Power/Interaction Model of Interpersonal Influence. 8 Analysis of Social Issues & Public Policy 1-22, 4 (2008).

[4]Bert H. Raven. The Bases of Power and the Power/Interaction Model of Interpersonal Influence. 8 Analysis of Social Issues & Public Policy 1-22, 4 (2008).

[5]Bert H. Raven. The Bases of Power and the Power/Interaction Model of Interpersonal Influence. 8 Analysis of Social Issues & Public Policy 1-22, 3 (2008).

[6]Bert H. Raven. The Bases of Power and the Power/Interaction Model of Interpersonal Influence. 8 Analysis of Social Issues & Public Policy 1-22, 4 (2008).

[7]Bert H. Raven. The Bases of Power and the Power/Interaction Model of Interpersonal Influence. 8 Analysis of Social Issues & Public Policy 1-22, 4 (2008).

sions and behave in ways that gains them access to the **Influencer's** expertise. Expert power depends upon the target believing that the person exerting the power knows best. It is a dependency power and may overlap with Formal Position power when the person in the higher position feels responsible to take care of the person in the lower position. This power is sometimes apparent in titles or degrees. It overlaps with the reputation aspect of Referent power.

Network Position power is the power of relationships and built on an ability to access the power of others. Network Position power is a consequence of "one of the most consistent findings in the social science literature . . . that who you know has a great deal to do with what you come to know."[8] Relationships are critical for obtaining information and accessing the power to collectively solve complex problems and execute complex tasks.

Power Bases

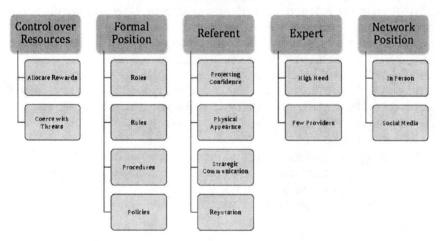

---

[8]Rob Cross, Stephen P. Borgatti, and Andrew Parker. Making Invisible Work Visible: Using Social Network Analysis to Support Strategic Collaboration, 44 California Management Review 25–46, 25 (2002).

The following sections offer a more detailed look at the various **Power Bases** and discuss options and strategies to develop and expand them. In particular, there are many opportunities for expanding and developing your Referent, Expert, and Network Position **Power Bases**.

§ 4:3 The Power Bases—Control over resources

Resources are anything that a **Target** wants or needs. Examples of resources are information, compensation and bonuses, budgetary allocations, a job, work assignments, career advancement opportunities, access to those in power, real estate, equipment, technology, social support, references, and clients. Reward power arises from one's ability to allocate resources. Coercive power arises from one's ability to withhold resources or punish a **Target**. The power is in issuing a promise of a reward or a threat of punitive action. The closer you are to controlling the resource, the more powerful you are. Determine the resources that you can develop personally or over which you can develop greater control. Information and empathy are resources that anyone can develop. People make decisions and act in ways that bring them benefits and allow them to avoid punishments, thus the promise of a benefit or the threat of a punishment can be a power to influence others' decisions and actions.

§ 4:4 The Power Bases—Formal position power

Formal position power arises from a formal position of authority within a particular organization or other system. It is "basically a combination of one's job title, job description, and prescribed responsibilities" providing the power "to control and direct" others. Essential ingredients are "selecting, evaluating, rewarding, and even terminating" others and controlling "merit increases, promotional opportunities, coveted job assignment, and vacation time."[1] One is empowered because of the formal role he or she holds within the system or as a result of the written word in documents adopted and empowered by the system. Lawyers are empowered to represent nonlawyers and provide legal advice. A partnership agreement in a law firm distributes decision-making power to specific roles. A parent has position power over his or her children, at least for a few years. A judge has position power in his or her courtroom. People defer to the

---

[Section 4:4]

[1]Larry E. Greiner and Virginia E. Schein. Power and Organization Development. 25–26 (1988).

requests or demands of a person with formal authority, thus an expressed want, need, or expectation by a person with authority over another can be a power to influence the others' decisions and actions.

§ 4:5   The Power Bases—Referent power

Referent power is the power of being likeable. Likeability as a point of influencing others was discussed in § 3:21. Referent power results from how a person presents oneself to the world and how others perceive that person. Not everyone finds the same qualities likeable in the same people; however, there seems to be a connection between the degree of Referent power that a person has and his or her projected confidence, physical appearance, and strategic communication skills. First impressions seem to weigh heavily and "[p]oor first impressions are avoidable."[1]

§ 4:6   The Power Bases—Referent power—Feeling confident

It is important to project confidence and self-assurance when you walk into a courtroom or a meeting, especially with someone new. Preparation seems to breed confidence. Mike Turner, "outworks the other guy." As a shareholder and senior attorney at Marshall Dennehey, Warner, Coleman & Goggin, with 26 years of litigation experience, Mike has tried in excess of 200 jury trials to verdict. He began his law career in the Philadelphia District Attorney's office. After trying numerous asbestos-related cases, he co-founded the firm of Kelley, Jasons, McGowan, Spinelli and Hanna in Philadelphia where he focused on the preparation and trial of complex personal injury, products liability, and criminal cases.[1] Diane Elderkin says that she is not supremely self-confident and to compensate, she prepares extensively for everything. "I lose a lot of sleep the night before a big argument but I prepare to the nth degree and it doesn't hurt." Another attorney interviewed likes to feel "so prepared that you don't even have to look at your notes, so that when you sit down, you speak

---

[Section 4:5]

[1]Anthony Tjan. Dear Entrepreneur: Avoid First Impression Mistakes. http://blogs.hbr.org/tjan/2010/11/dear-entrepreneur-avoid-first-.html?referral=00563&cm__mmc=email-__-newsletter-__-daily__alert-__- (last visited November 24, 2010).

[Section 4:6]

[1]http://www.marshalldennehey.com/Bio/MichaelTurner.asp (last visited March 24, 2011).

with authority." Gathering as much information as is possible about a person or situation before the first meeting develops confidence and reduces anxiety.

If you feel confident, you can spend more energy in choosing the right behaviors to project confidence in your physical appearance and strategic communication. These choices may include where you position yourself in a room, how and when you make direct eye contact, and what you say and how you say it.

The MBTI® mentioned in § 2:9 as a useful tool for understanding different preferences in gathering data is also a useful tool for understanding differences that make some people appear to be more confident and likeable. Another dichotomy in the MBTI® is the distinction between Extraversion and Introversion. Extraverts have an advantage in appearing confident because they often know a lot of people, are perceived as approachable and easily engaged, like networking and talking to many people, are outgoing, and their energy tends to increase as conversation develops.[2]

Judge C. Darnell Jones II sits on the United States District Court for the Eastern District of Pennsylvania and in addition to his intellect, warmth, and emotional intelligence, he is an Extravert. His office is filled with myriad pictures of family members and friends and letters from people whose lives he has touched interspersed with the news stories, plaques, and awards that tell the story of his professional development and personal life in connection with other people. Prior to the Federal Bench he served on the Court of Common Pleas for the First Judicial District of Pennsylvania for 21 years. Running for re-election was part of that job. He became the President Judge of that Court before being appointed to the Federal Bench. This type of career is nearly impossible without an ability to project confidence; Judge Jones has additional Referent Power because he projects a combination of confidence, competence, and warmth.

§ 4:7 The Power Bases—Referent power—Physical appearance

Physical appearance and presence contributes to one's Referent Power. Debating the fairness or ethics of this phenomenon is not the purpose of this book. Similar to the existence of implicit biases, it is a fact. It exists, and to develop and expand one's **Power Bases** and **Influence Strategies**, an **Influencer** must address its presence. Physical appearance includes: the clothing, hairstyle, accessories, and makeup a person wears; how and

---

[2]Otto Kroeger & Janet M. Thuesen. Type Talk 17, 18, 65 (1988).

where that person positions and uses his or her body, including height, posture, and gesture; and how and when a person uses his or her voice. Every tall lawyer interviewed for this book pointed to his or her height as a source of power. Height is a privilege. One lawyer of color, who was interviewed, mentioned the need to be conscious of the unfortunate implicit biases that required the additional consideration of how to avoid inadvertently undermining power by using voice and emotions in a way that would decrease that person's ability to be influential. Being a person of color, like being a woman or a person with a physical disability, is being in a less-privileged and subordinated position before that person's requests are ever evaluated on their merits. A **Target's** thinking and emotions are affected by an **Influencer's** actions that affect the five senses of the **Target**, which create an immediate bias in favor or against the **Influencer**. Everything has the potential to matter to a **Target**: the auditory impact of your voice, clothing, and shoes; the olfactory impact of your body wash, shampoo, or fragrance; the physical distance between the **Influencer** and **Target**; and the visual impact of one's clothing, hand gestures, and body postures.

§ 4:8   The Power Bases—Referent power—Strategic communication

Referent power also appears in what one says and how one says it, what one does not say, and how people listen and express empathy. In Chapter 2 the influence that stories have on our thinking, feeling, and behavior was explained. Stories are extremely powerful influencers. Some stories are privileged in the sense of being widely told and believed, while others are not. The people with power to privilege their stories can have a tremendous impact on constructing reality. For instance, the power that created the leadership performance models explained in § 3:10 assigned positive attributes to agentic behaviors. Agentic behavior favors male leaders because of implicit bias. There was power behind the choice to create a leadership-performance model based on research subjects with stay-at-home wives. There was power to elevate the research to a story with meaning beyond the specific variables in the research. A group of people decided to publish the original research and another group decided to use the research as a measure of good leadership. Finding the power to be able to convey your stories with the right words, in the right way, to the right people so that it becomes privileged is critical. The groups within your organization responsible for making decisions about promotion, bonuses, and performance evaluations need to know your stories and be positively affected in their thinking and feeling about you as a result. You are responsible for creating those stories and making sure that they are heard by the right people. That's referent power.

"Power constructs reality."[1] The language of lawyers is a language of power. When one uses the language of lawyers to construct a story of reality, one uses a language of rights, entitlement, acquisition, ownership, possession, obligations, liability, fault, guilt, ownership, possession, division, and coercion. "[L]egal tales ... constitute a language of power."[2] Expect that stories using legal jargon may inadvertently trigger unhelpful responses in the person hearing or reading those stories. Remember the discussion about how people tend to react to power. The negative reaction that some people have to power may engender bad feelings and ultimately negative judgments in reaction to a story that is intended to make someone more likeable but uses the legal language of power. It is difficult to convince a person to conclude that you build collaborative relationships if the language you use reminds them of the language of lawyers. It is difficult to construct a story about collaboration or connection using the language of law. Consider how this idiosyncratic language affects likeability and Referent Power.

The language we use can create or undermine our referent power. Which response is more powerful: to say, "let me finish" or "can I continue?" Does it depend on the context? Contrast your use of language with opposing counsel at a deposition and your use of language with a client. Before you choose your words, consider your intended outcome and the feeling in the other that you intend to evoke.

Referent power is also expressed in how you say what you say. Voice is one part of appearance that can be changed within a certain range, from pace of speech, volume, and words emphasized. In addition, the tone used can be modulated with coaching and practice. Dean Epps advises one to develop an

---

[Section 4:8]

[1]Allan C. Hutchinson. Part of an Essay on Power and Interpretation (with Suggestions on how to make Bouillabasse), 60 New York University Law Review 851, 877 http://osgoode.yorku.ca/osgmedia.nsf/0/C921A65EE6A854D9852571C 4006150CC/$FILE/Part%20of%20an%20Essay%20on%20Power%20and%20Inte rpretation.pdf (last visited March 5, 2011) (1985).

[2]Allan C. Hutchinson. Part of an Essay on Power and Interpretation (with Suggestions on how to make Bouillabasse), 60 New York University Law Review 851, 872 http://osgoode.yorku.ca/osgmedia.nsf/0/C921A65EE6A854D9852571C 4006150CC/$FILE/Part%20of%20an%20Essay%20on%20Power%20and%20Inte rpretation.pdf (last visited March 5, 2011) (1985).

awareness of this and more. She suggests thinking about how one's speech sounds, irrespective of the content. Is there an inadvertent sing-song intonation, mumbling or grumbling, or a question tone imposed on statements? In a conversational flow, an interruption is an exercise of power as is the response to the interruption. Speaking with notes usually is less powerful than speaking without notes.[3] Pausing for emphasis or giving the listener a moment to catch up can be highly influential in precipitating thinking in connection with what was immediately before the pause. People seem to find alliteration, lists of three, contrasting words pairs, humor, and short declarative sentences more alluring and easier to listen to. Some research suggests that "expressing anger is usually more effective than expressing sadness, guilt, or remorse in being seen as powerful."[4] However, when expressing anger, there may be implicit biases that create obstacles because of your gender, race, or other social identity characteristic.

As explained in Chapter 3, the emotional states of the **Influencer** and **Target** affect the effectiveness of the **Influence Strategy.** Emotional states, including energy, are contagious. "[L]ong-term emotional states can spread between socially connected individuals."[5] Choose language and behaviors that lead "those with power [to] enhance their positive feelings about themselves" since people "seek out positive information and avoid negative feedback."[6] Flattery might just create likeability and prime the social norm of reciprocity.[7] If you ask someone for help, offer an explanation of why you have selected that particular person. If you point out a problem, do so in way that does not undermine the person's competence or sense of self-worth.[8] Mirroring behavior or literally pointing out similarities works because people "prefer those who are similar."[9]

Although people are naturally drawn to and want to help those whom they perceive to be similar to them, there are two caveats. First, people also want to be recognized and appreciated for who

---

[3]Jeffrey Pfeffer. Power 142–45 (2010).

[4]Jeffrey Pfeffer. Power 128 (2010).

[5]Allison L. Hill, David G. Rand, Martin A. Nowak, and Nicholas A. Christakis. Emotions as Infectious Diseases in a Large Social Network: the SISa Model. Royal Society Publishing http://rspb.royalsocietypublishing.org/content/early/2010/07/03/rspb.2010.1217.full (last visited March 5, 2010).

[6]Jeffrey Pfeffer. Power 31 (2010).

[7]Jeffrey Pfeffer. Power 33 (2010).

[8]Jeffrey Pfeffer. Power 33 (2010).

[9]Jeffrey Pfeffer. Power 31–32 (2010).

they are and their differences. This is part of inclusion strategies to eliminate bias and improve innovation. It is also at the heart of social justice. Second, people are not attracted to the similarities in others unless they also like and value that part of themselves. Remember § 3:25 and the Unconscious Blockers that might be present. When a person sees a disliked part of himself or herself in you, the person is less likely to be helpful to or positively influenced by you. The best action in this situation might be to become a Wanderer and look for a more hospitable context or become curious about what is motivating that person to respond irrationally. What do you say or do to help others feel good about themselves, want to treat you well and help you, and show connection and similarity?

Targets who feel a positive emotional reaction as a result of an interaction with an **Influencer** are more likely to be influenced. It should be clear that most people who have the power to make a positive difference in your life will want to be around you and help you if they leave an encounter feeling happy rather than sad, angry, or intimated. Indeed, people are universally and immediately assessed on their warmth and competence while intelligence is susceptible to being measured by a person's toughness or even meanness.[10] No doubt this is like walking on a tightrope and a positive outcome is more likely if you spend time learning what works for you and balancing your behavior as a result.

Finally, there will be times when speaking will not be the best **Influence Strategy**. Therefore, "learn the unfamiliar skill of being good listeners."[11] Improving your ability to listen empathetically and provide effective feedback will increase your likeability and Referent Power. Identify the behaviors to use to communicate empathy and understanding of someone else's perspective. Unfortunately, some people have "difficulty putting themselves in the other's place" because they are "so smart [that] they can't understand why others don't get it." Often these people do not realize that "intelligence can be intimidating."[12] The MBTI® Extraversion preference can become a problem when an intel-

---

[10]Jeffrey Pfeffer. Power 87 (2010).

[11]Allan C. Hutchinson. Part of an Essay on Power and Interpretation (with Suggestions on how to make Bouillabasse), 60 New York University Law Review 851, 873 http://osgoode.yorku.ca/osgmedia.nsf/0/C921A65EE6A854D9852571C4006150CC/$FILE/Part%20of%20an%20Essay%20on%20Power%20and%20Interpretation.pdf (last visited March 5, 2011) (1985).

[12]Jeffrey Pfeffer. Power 56 (2010).

ligent extravert has difficulty being silent. Introverts, on the other hand, are generally perceived as very good listeners.[13]

Mike Turner knows that physical appearance matters and that being tall and having a deep voice works to his advantage as a trial lawyer. He also knows that often at least one juror is noticing and judging every suit, shirt, and tie that he wears during a trial, regardless of the length of the trial. He is an outstanding trial lawyer for his clients because of his obvious competence and physical appearance, but equally because he is easy to get along with, a very good listener, and tremendously empathetic. Mike is also a positive, upbeat optimist and people gravitate toward him because of that, too. He has "chosen to be a happy person." When he thinks about the reason behind any person's decisions, he thinks about the person holistically—who are they, what have they experienced in their lives, and what are the issues presently in their lives? People tend to like him, want to listen to him, and want to work with him.

Perceptions of whether someone is likeable will vary. Carrie Hogan's advice is to "stay true to who you are; people smell a phony. If you are trying to act, dress, or talk like someone you are not, they pick up on that." Carrie says that she is not always perfect, polished, or politically correct, but she believes that people experience her as believable and genuine. She has her own style, which is attractive, confident, and genuine. It is not the way Alecia Florrick, the main character in the television show The Good Wife, dresses and speaks. The **Influence Strategy** to convince someone who is primed to think that a woman lawyer is likeable if she is looks, talks, and dresses like Alecia may require adjustment, since none of the women lawyers that I know are beautiful actresses with sultry voices whose dialogue is provided by a professional writer.

Worksheet: Expanding Your Referent Power Base

Use the table below to chart your present use of Referent Power and develop an action plan to expand current or develop new areas of your Referent **Power Base**. Action plans may include skill building through workshops, programs, coaching, and practice plans.

---

[13]Otto Kroeger & Janet M. Thuesen, Type Talk 19 (1988).

My Referent Power Base: Creating Likeability

Projecting Confidence	Physical Appearance	Strategic Communication
For each event and your role and responsibilities in that event, what prework do you do to feel fully prepared? This can be before a meeting, court appearance or deposition, formal presentation, mediation, or negotiation? I prepare by . . .	What do you think about to manage your physical appearance? Do you think about: • Clothing • Accessories • Hair • Posture • Gestures • Fragrances • Shoes • Nails • Voice • Your body placement in relation to others	How do you use strategic communication to create the appearance that you want?
Fill in the blank: In the moment of each event above, I project confidence by . . .	What do you do to create the physical appearance that you want to project? How do you adjust each of the following: • Clothing • Accessories • Hair • Posture • Gestures • Fragrances • Shoes • Nails • Voice • Your body placement in relation to others	Strategic Communication Considerations: • Language used • Ideas conveyed • Emotions you convey and affect in others, anger and warmth in particular • Listening • Expressing empathy • Giving feedback effectively • Conveying dominance and assertiveness • Use of interruptions • Use of pauses

Projecting Confidence	Physical Appearance	Strategic Communication
What do you do to use or expand your MBTI® Extraversion side to project confidence?		What do you do to use or expand your MBTI® Introversion side to project interest through listening?
What do you do to manage your emotional and social intelligence in the moment to project confidence?		What do you do to manage your emotional and social intelligence in the moment?

Worksheet: Planning to Use Your Referent Power for First Impressions[14]

If you are about to meet a **Target** (anyone who ought to have a positive impression of you) for the first time, consider the following questions carefully and provide written answers before a first meeting:

1. After a Google search, what did you learn about the **Target** and the **Target's** organization? What did you learn from your online activities about the **Target's** current and relevant needs, wants, and expectations?

   _____

   _____

   _____

2. Did you find an online image of the **Target**?
3. Where did you go for your online searches in addition to Google?

   _____

   _____

   _____

4. Have you located people to ask about the **Target's** current wants, needs, and expectations? Where have you looked, who have you located, and what have you learned?

   _____

   _____

   _____

5. What are your objectives for the meeting? What do you intend

---

[14]Adapted from Anthony Tjan. Dear Entrepreneur: Avoid First Impression Mistakes. http://blogs.hbr.org/tjan/2010/11/dear-entrepreneur-avoid-first-.html?referral=00563&cm__mmc=email-__-newsletter-__-daily__alert-__- (last visited November 24, 2010).

to say or do in preparation for or at the meeting to achieve your objectives?

_____

_____

_____

_____

6. What sources of Referent Power will you use, to what end, and how in preparation for the meeting and at the meeting?

_____

_____

_____

_____

§ 4:9 The Power Bases—Expert power

Expert power is relative and based on a dependency relationship. A **Target** lacks the expertise and depends on the **Influencer** to provide a scarce resource that he or she strongly wants or needs. The degree of power depends on the rarity of the knowledge or skill, the difference in knowledge or ability between the **Influencer** and the **Target**, and the **Target's** level of want or need. The knowledge or skill constitutes a valuable resource over which the possessor has exclusive access and control. For example, a lawyer has a good deal of expert power and can be quite influential in using that power to influence someone who "does not possess a similar expertise."[1] A lawyer can be expert in an area of law that is at the top of the value pyramid, like bet-the-company litigation. Lawyers with a reputation for a niche expertise are sought after and offered presentation and publications opportunities. Seizing these opportunities expands the lawyer's exposure to potential clients, employers, and other career opportunities. The increased exposure also strengthens the lawyer's reputation, i.e., the perception of the lawyer as an expert.

For some lawyers, the feeling of being an expert—the "go-to" person—is itself a feeling of happiness and success. Gary Levin is a partner and member of the policy committee at the Intellectual Property boutique law firm of Woodcock Washburn. Success and happiness for Gary comes from being the "go-to" guy in his law firm. The "feeling of proficiency" in what he does and enjoyment of the "academics and strategy of it" is empowering for him. He is

---

[Section 4:9]

[1]Larry E. Greiner and Virginia E. Schein. Power and Organization Development. 28 (1998).

appreciated and respected for his legal knowledge in his firm and likes to be asked for his opinion, views, and help. When one of his partners was working with a young associate and needed to know the name of a case, he called on Gary and said to the associate, "I want to show you some of the cheapest legal research available to us." That is the essence of Expert Power for a lawyer and when having the expertise also brings happiness and feelings of success to a lawyer, the **Power Base** expands naturally.

A lawyer can also develop expertise in delivering a unique and valuable attorney-client relationship experience. Each expertise is valuable and powerful. What can you do to create a niche expertise? What can you do to create a unique and highly valued experience for your clients?

§ 4:10   The Power Bases—Network position power

The effectiveness of any action plan, including an **Influence Strategy** depends on information, opportunities, and ability. The plan's designer will create the action steps of the plan based on information about the wants, needs, and expectations of all of the people affected by the plan. The plan's design, to reach its intended goals, will depend on the available opportunities to reach the goals. The effectiveness of the design and its implementation depend on the skill level of anyone who has a role in executing the plan. Each person has limited knowledge and skills. Borrowing words from Gary Levin, in a world where "complacency doesn't work, complacency isn't a strategy," every person's networks expand his or her knowledge and available skills to use in the design and implementation of any action plan. Influencing anyone beyond one's direct connections happens because of one's Network Position Power.

Networks are the departments, social and professional groups, offices, organizations, and online groups in which one has membership. Membership means that a person is part of the group. The deeper the connection within the group, the more power one will derive from that network, up to a point. Networks help a person identify opportunities, gather critical information, form coalitions, develop mentoring and sponsorship relationships, and find a safety net of support. Network power "is cultivated over the years, and later becomes the Old Boy's/Girl's Network."[1] It is a source from which one can expand one's **Power Bases** by

---

[Section 4:10]

[1]Larry E. Greiner and Virginia E. Schein. Power and Organization Development. 31 (1998).

virtue of having access to the **Power Bases** of others. A Network is a multiplier. It expands one's **Power Bases** and **Influence Strategies** to a richer and more robust level.

One's network is "positively related to obtaining good performance evaluations, objective measures of career success such as salary and organizational level, and subjective attitudes assessing career satisfaction and important for people's careers, period."[2] It works because it "brings you into contact with more people and keeps you in contact with them, thereby increasing the chances that when they need advice, want to find an investment partners, or are thinking of a candidate for some positions, they will remember you." It is also a shared ability of linked agents to alter their environment in ways advantageous to these agents individually and collectively."[3] Networks have the potential for leveling the playing field and creating inclusion for groups generally marginalized by privileging the network itself.

One's networks may overlap. Some networks comprise professional acquaintances and others comprise friends or family. The people in one's networks are sources of information about **Targets**, opportunities, and oneself. **Influencers** who are trying to learn more about themselves and how others perceive them might approach members of their networks for personal feedback. Networks are connections to other people. Networks are alive and need to be developed and maintained by regular contact with the members. The type and frequency of contact will vary depending upon circumstances and includes e-mail, telephone calls, handwritten cards and notes, and in-person meetings. Develop your networks intentionally based upon your personal vision for success and happiness and your specific goals.[4]

Leadership networks are growing in importance. These networks "provide resources and support for leaders, and increase the scope and scale of impact leaders can have individually and collectively."[5] People in peer leadership groups:

> provide each other with trusted and relevant information, advice, and support [and are a source of opportunities for] speaking at each other's event, trading or providing services, getting quick reliable information to a question . . . providing each other with leads to

---

[2]Jeffrey Pfeffer. Power 110 (2010).

[3]David E. Booher and Judith E. Innes. Network Power in Collaborative Planning, 21 Journal of Planning Education and Research 221, 225 (2002).

[4]Keith Ferrazzi. Never Eat Alone 30 (2005).

[5]Bruce Hoppe and Claire Reinelt. Social Network Analysis and the Evaluation of Leadership Networks 21 The Leadership Quarterly 600–619, 600 (2010).

new job opportunities and job references . . . introducing each other to people in each other's networks, [and] joint inquiry or collaborations. [Interestingly,] [c]areer success correlates strongly to one's position in the informal [organizational leadership] network [and] the time one spends networking informally. . .whereas the time one spends convening more formally (e.g., meetings) can actually be counter-productive. (Internal citations omitted.)[6]

Mike Turner emphasizes the importance of building one's networks, joining Boards, and interacting with people. He advises being assertive and getting to know every person on the Board and identifying people in a position to assign work. He also reminds attorneys that because it is impossible to know who will be in a position and willing to help you in the future, whatever you do, meet more people and let them know what you do and what you need.

Worksheet: Developing Networks

Answer the following questions.

1. Given your vision of success, goals, and passions in life; who or which groups, in general or specific terms, do you need or want to meet? Why?
   a. Do you need mentors and sponsors?
   b. Do you need someone who will give you honest feedback about your strengths and weaknesses?
   c. Do you need industry connections? If so, which industries?
   d. Do you need people in positions to publicize who you are and what you do?
   e. Do you need speaking or writing opportunities?
   f. Do you need emotional support?
   g. Do you need to have more fun?
2. Where can you go to meet the people and join the groups that will help satisfy your needs and wants?
3. What can you do to strengthen connections with individuals?
   a. What do you want or need from each individual?
   b. What does each individual need or want?
   c. What can you offer to each individual?
4. What can you do to strengthen your position within a particular network?
   a. What do you know about the network? Is it a formal or informal network? What are its needs and wants?

---

[6]Bruce Hoppe and Claire Reinelt. Social Network Analysis and the Evaluation of Leadership Networks 21 The Leadership Quarterly 600–619, 607 (2010).

b. What can you offer to each network?
5. How will you use your Referent and/or Expert Power to strengthen your relationships and network positions?
6. Identify a specific opportunity to strengthen a relationship or network position and create an action plan using your other **Power Bases**.

Case Study: Nancy—Referent and Network Power

Nancy is a partner and the Chair of the Labor and Employment Practice group at regional law firm with offices in the Northeastern United States. After leaving a large firm with an international presence to follow her family to a location outside of a major metropolitan area, she joined a very small, local boutique labor and employment firm, but soon found that the size was not a good fit for her. One of her former colleagues was practicing with a regional office of her current law firm and through him, she met the managing partner of the regional office and then the managing partner of the large metropolitan office.

She was invited to join the firm's local office in a Counsel position and, in addition to practicing employment law, developed a niche practice representing colleges and universities, which began with a single small liberal arts college and a very challenging legal situation. The situation required her to be accessible to them "24/7," which she was. Eventually, a favorable result was reached. Subsequently, the college retained Nancy in different areas—tenure denial, student plagiarism, and discrimination cases. She was retained by a second private school, then another, and then an insurer of educational institutions retained her. Now she has a niche reputation and many more colleges and universities as clients. This isn't the only way that Nancy has grown her practice.

Nancy learned that "you cannot predict where the next new client will come from." She enjoys running and joined a group of women that runs together. While running with the group one day, one of the women, who was not an attorney, mentioned that she knew of a small college that was seeking new counsel; Nancy's running friend offered to make an introduction and with this introduction, Nancy developed a major client.

Nancy attributes her rainmaking success to three factors: (1) her comprehensive knowledge of her practice area; (2) the quality of her work product and services; and (3) being accessible to her clients. In her words, "I want to develop a relationship with my clients so that they trust and rely on me."

Her growing practice was followed by her firm's leadership asking that she seek partnership, which she did. Two years after becoming a partner, she was asked to chair the Labor and Employment Practice Group. In her leadership role as Chair, she is responsible to develop and grow the practice group and work closely with the firm's other practice groups to cross-market and integrate their clients and services.

Nancy is very aware of how she uses her Referent **Power Base**. Her goal is to gain power in any situation. She is aware of every aspect of her physical appearance and that it matters—her hair, nails, shoes, and clothing. This doesn't mean she thinks this is fair or right. She accepts this and intends to look professional every time. Her awareness of her appearance doesn't stop there.

When she walks into a room, her goal, when appropriate for the context, is to "take control of the environment." Control, to Nancy, doesn't mean talking right away or acting in an aggressive manner. It means "waiting for the right moment to speak" and speaking in a way that has the impact she wants. She may speak in a quiet voice from the start or "build to a crescendo and then drop to a quiet voice."

In one very complex matter involving several different lawyers representing different claims and pieces of litigation, Nancy was the lead employment lawyer. She was attending a meeting, the goal of which was to reach a global settlement in the matter. She walked into the conference room and immediately noticed a sea of suits and ties. She sat down quietly, not at the head of the table, and waited for the meeting to begin, at which time everyone turned to her to begin the meeting. That was an "aha" moment for her. She realized that she had developed a level of control and influence in that room. Throughout the case, Nancy had taken a lead position on the claim that she was defending and in how that claim related to the other pieces of the litigation. She ultimately became the designated leader. Nancy prepared for this case in her typical manner, which is to be "so prepared that you don't have to look at your notes, and when you sit down, you speak with authority." She is driven "to be the best that [she] can be, to be recognized as a success, and to [be] the winning and prevailing party."

In that same matter, one of her co-counsel related comments made about her when she was out of the conference room. One of the attorneys commented, "What's with her? Does ice flow through her veins?" Another attorney responded by referring to Nancy as the "ice queen." Nancy relates that when she heard those words, she controlled her emotional reaction by "breathing through it, literally focusing on [her] stomach expanding and contracting" with each breath. She also reflected on the comments and later concluded that in that particular context, an adversarial setting, it was a positive moniker because it "showed control and influence."

In contrast to the litigation setting, when Nancy is in her office, despite possibly having strong opinions on how the office should be managed or personnel matters resolved, has "learned to listen to others express their view and compare and contrast everyone's views, including [her] own." If she has an idea, she will "try to raise questions in a quiet, respectful way to integrate [her] thoughts into the group." She acknowledges that "it doesn't always work." In this context, Nancy believes that "it is not her position to be the leader" in an office matter when someone else is the managing partner. Instead, it is her position to express her views in a collegial, collaborative way.

Questions

1. Which **Power Bases** did Nancy use at different times? Why was each one an effective choice?
2. How do you explain the "ice queen" comments and being selected as the leader?
3. Where do you notice the use of multiple **Power Bases** simultaneously?

Case Study: Nikki Johnson-Huston—Identifying Power Bases and Influence Strategies

Nikki Johnson-Huston has a vision. She wants to be inspirational and change the world for people who grew up like her. As she says, "most people think that it would not be possible to do what I'm doing now"; however, she will tell you that her "disadvantages have turned out to make [her] better and stronger." She was homeless as a child and without an intact family as a support system. She now lives her dream of being a lawyer. She attended college at night, while working full time as a nanny during the day, but failed out of college the first time. In the span of four years, she earned a J.D., M.B.A., and L.L.M. in taxation. She is in her early 30s and works as an Assistant City Solicitor for the City of Philadelphia. Her pathway to success followed her waking up one morning and realizing that she was holding on to a lot of anger because of the unfairness in her life. She realized that her history only made it harder, not impossible, for her to realize her dream. Her disadvantages, she says, "have turned out to make [her] better, stronger."

Nikki was named as one of the Philadelphia Business Journal's "Women of Distinction," one of the "10 Under 40 to Watch" by the

Philadelphia Tribune, and "A Star of the Quarter" by the American Bar Association in 2010. In 2009, she was selected by The Legal Intelligencer as one of 30 lawyers "on the Fast Track," and also received the Craig M. Perry Award from the Philadelphia Bar Association for her substantial community service work. Nikki has accomplished her dream of becoming a lawyer and now has a revised vision of her future. She expects that children will be part of her future. She thinks that perhaps she will have a best-selling book within five to 10 years and/or be hosting a talk show. She is certain that it will be "in the legal realm." She wants "to influence other women because a lot of women are not living the life that they want to live."

Nikki is quite clear about what she wants and how she thinks, She "like[s] how power sounds." This is different from many other people who respond to the idea of power in a fearful way. Her words conveyed more than a goal; they suggested a value to "use power in a positive way" to have "control over [one's] destiny." She has "no problem saying what she wants."

Nikki has power and uses it in a variety of ways. She "like[s] to collect relationships" and "know[s] that as an African American woman if I play my cards right, there are a lot of doors open to me. There are a lot of people who want to help people like me if I am open to it." When she thinks about relationships, she thinks about making people feel inspired, heard, respected, and "good enough." To inspire people, she talks about "the bigger picture" so that others "feel like they can make a difference." Then collectively they have something to work on together. To make people feel heard and respected, she acts consistently with her words and follows through on her promises. She also pays attention to:

> a person's circumstances, how they fit in at their organization, and the pressures on them. Often they are not talking for themselves but for a larger company and the message they bring back to the company may be that they have to pay the City money. I try to make an outcome that they feel heard and respected.

Further, she explains her decisions. If she has to decline a request for her time, she will "explain why [she] can't give it the time and attention it deserves" and suggests that the person try again later and maybe she will have the time then. She has discovered that giving a reason makes a difference in how someone feels about the exchange.

She thinks about her image. "I do a good job managing how people see me and it's not accidental." She wants them to notice that she is smart, competent, attractive, and will follow through on her promises. She accepts that people can't see how hard she works. She recognizes that she looks younger than her actual age and gets pushed aside because of that appearance. She tells people what she is doing rather than assuming that they will know or that they won't find it important.

Despite her best efforts, Nikki knows that not everyone will like her and "having influence sometimes makes you a target." She has learned "to roll with the punches and not take things personally." If something doesn't work, she is "clear on what is [her] stuff and what is their stuff" and will "move on to the next thing [because] the world rewards that mindset. Further she says that if she makes a "mistake, then [she will] correct it. Most things can be undone."

Managing her emotions isn't easy. She is passionate and has "a quick tongue." She's recognized that as a young, African-American woman, "going form zero to sixty won't work to my advantage." She tries to take a moment and ask herself whether doing so with get her where she wants to be or make an enemy. That said, if she "make[s] a mistake," she will apologize. She says that she is lucky to have a great husband, who is also a great sounding board. "If I want to flip out or cry, I do it at home."

Questions: Answer the following questions with as much specificity from the case study as possible.

1. What motivating factors work to Nikki's advantage? How and why?
2. Identify the different **Power Bases** and how she uses them.
3. Which decision-making processes is she thinking about and how does she adjust her behavior because of them?

§4:11 The Power Bases—Network position power— Focusing your efforts to increase your Power Bases

There has been a shift in the professional and personal wants, needs, and expectations of the younger generation of lawyers. They may lack the economic privilege to hire enough help to support a smoothly running personal life. The likelihood of having a stay-at-home spouse is lower than was historically the case. Loyalty to a single employer has diminished. The benefits of partnership in a law firm seem less clear to many. Additionally, client loyalty has decreased with the increase of new economic and performance pressures on in-house counsel. One consequence is that the strength in the Control over Resources and Formal Position **Power Bases** is lessened. As the Wanderer archetype increases in use by lawyers and clients, Referent, Expert, and Network Position **Power Bases** become more important. The good news is that increasing those **Power Bases**, which are growing in importance, is possible with self-reflection, planning, and practice.

The best way to increase the effectiveness of any **Power Base** is to begin by assessing your available **Power Bases**. Inventory your current **Power Bases** by identifying each **Power Base** and your attributes, characteristics, or resources that fit within it.

Worksheet: Evaluating Your Power Bases

Fill in the chart.

Power Base	My Attributes, Characteristics, and/or Resources	Gaps
Control Over Resources	I control these resources:	I am missing these resources:
Formal Position	I hold these positions:	I could hold these positions:
Referent	Likeability:	There is room for improvement here:
Expert	These are areas of expertise that I have that are rare and in demand:	I could develop these areas of expertise:

Power Base	My Attributes, Characteristics, and/or Resources	Gaps
Network Position	These are my networks:	I would like to have networks that could do this for me:

After you have inventoried your **Power Bases**, consider how to fill in the gaps. Develop a list of ways to increase your **Power Bases**. Can you increase your knowledge and skill level to expand your Expert **Power Base**? Do you control or can you develop a resource, including how you spend your time, which could be disbursed in a way to improve any of your **Power Bases**? Are there people who could help you develop a **Power Base**? Do you know which written procedures and policies control decisions that are important to your career? Do you understand how they work and what you must do to help yourself? Can you build on your existing sources of Referent Power and add new sources? In which networks should you develop a stronger position?

Power Base	Strategy to Increase Power Base	Use of Power Base in Strategy
Control over Resources	• Advance your career and increase your control over valuable resources with the authority that comes from a higher formal position	• Trade favors, give guarantees, bestow resources, or make promises and threats

Power Base	Strategy to Increase Power Base	Use of Power Base in Strategy
	• Remember that knowledge, time, access to opportunities and people, and anything else that someone wants or needs are resources	
	• Develop your skills for identifying the powerful decision-makers and developing deep relationships for internal and external sponsorship that will lead to client development and career advancement? Learn what the decision-makers want, need, and expect then be able to satisfy those wants, needs, and expectations	
	• Learn what the decision-makers want, need, and expect then be able to satisfy those wants, needs, and expectations	
	• Identify pairings of people in your networks for mutually beneficial relationships, sponsor relationships, or mentoring relationships	

Power Base	Strategy to Increase Power Base	Use of Power Base in Strategy
Formal Position	• Advance your position by knowing the written and unwritten rules, policies, procedures, and culture for advancing • Develop sponsorship relationships with the powerful decision-makers • Develop an awareness of the relevant political dynamics	• Directing subordinates in organization or association to take desired action
Referent Power	• Collect data on how you present yourself to others in various situations from casual meetings to formal meetings and presentations. What do do well and where are the gaps? Fill in the gaps and develop your strategic communication and influence skills using words, voice, physical presence, appearance, and body language effectively. • Develop your emotional and social intelligence and ability to manage stress	• Use your skills in effective listening and giving and getting feedback to increase your likability, gather important data, and prime your Target to increase the likelihood that decisions will be made in your favor. • Use your skills for designing and executing strategy to address roadblocks and find alternate pathways to your goals or including negotiating a solution

Power Base	Strategy to Increase Power Base	Use of Power Base in Strategy
	• Develop your conflict tolerance and response skills	• Use your knowledge of political dynamics to obtain the assistance of key decision makers' and their peers
	• Develop your comfort with mistakes and change your perspective on mistakes	• Use your sense of timing, tenacity and patience to stay focused on your goals and make strategic choices of when and how to attempt to influence decisions
		• Use mistakes as learning opportunities to revise and improve your strategies
Expert Power	• Build a reputation as an expert through publishing and speaking opportunities	• Let your reputation work for you.
	• Become an expert in a niche area (subject matter or geographic location or delivery of services)	• Discredit opposition or competitors if appropriate directly or through the use of network power of others
		• Use niche expertise to build a referral network with others in different niches
Network Position	• Form alliances and coalitions to increase power reach	• Use networks, alliances, and coalitions to influence political decision-making

Power Base	Strategy to Increase Power Base	Use of Power Base in Strategy
	• Join and become active in those networks that you have identifies as comprising the people who can influence the decisions that matter to you	• Use as referral networks for opportunities and sponsorship relationships
	• Use social media networks to collect data and as first steps to building deeper relationships	• Use networks to get important information about the decision-makers who matter to you
	• Create new networks around share interests	• Use networks for support and finding/building mutually beneficial relationships within those networks
	• Surround yourself with competent others	• Use your network power to find out about and get appointed to the career-making work assignments or business development opportunities including client pitch-teams, Boards, social events, speaking, and publishing opportunities, and pro bono work.
		• Use your network power to get into more powerful networks

§ 4:12   **Chapter summary**

- **Power Bases** are an **Influencer's** potential for influencing a **Target.**
- The five **Power Bases** are: (1) Control over Resources; (2) Formal Position; (3) Expert; (4) Referent; and (5) Network Position.
- The best opportunities for expanding your personal power are to develop your Expert, Referent, and Network Position **Power Bases**.

Chapter 5

Influence Strategies

> **KeyCite®:** Cases and other legal materials listed in KeyCite Scope can be researched through the KeyCite service on Westlaw®. Use KeyCite to check citations for form, parallel references, prior and later history, and comprehensive citator information, including citations to other decisions and secondary materials.

§ 5:1   Chapter focus: How we got to this point and where we are going from here

With an understanding of one's personal goals and ideas of success, insight, and control over one's thinking about power, influence, conflict, and challenges, knowledge about how people and groups make decisions, and access into one's personal **Power Bases**, it is possible to develop general and specific **Influence Strategies** to move oneself closer to one's personal goals and ideas of success. This chapter explains strategy, action plans, **Influence Strategies**, the Action Learning process, and specific **Influence Strategies** that will be useful in any action plan to reach one's goals and create one's vision of a successful and happy personal and professional life.

Influence Strategies are action plans designed with steps to affect the decision-making and behavior of a **Target** in ways that the **Influencer** thinks will bring about an intended outcome and move the **Influencer** closer to his or her goals. An Action Plan, which is a series of steps or actions for advancing toward a goal, is only as good as the data on which it is based and the better the data, the better the design. When an **Influencer** implements an Action Plan using an Action Learning orientation, he or she is reflecting on his or her actions and experiences and analyzing their usefulness in moving toward the Action Plan's goal. The analysis and conclusions are new and better data for the next iteration of the Action Plan. The new data may pertain to the **Influencer**, the **Target**, and/or the context of the **Influence Strategy** used and certainly pertains to what worked well and what did not. Perhaps you will discover a need to develop one or more of your **Power Bases** or to Wander into a new context. Perhaps you will find out that what your **Target** needs, wants, and expects is something different from that which you and even the **Target** had thought. Iterative Action Plans improve in their effectiveness over time.

§ 5:2   The smart play: Changing your hidden mindsets and embracing Action Learning

There are three big obstacles for lawyers who want to embrace an Action Learning mindset and each is embedded in they way lawyers think. First, lawyers tend to think that mistakes should be avoided at all costs. This risk-averse thinking will be an obstacle. Second, lawyers tend to believe that there is always a single truth provable with the best advocacy. Thinking that there is a single, correct strategy that anyone can use to reach his or her goals will be an obstacle. This thinking creates a dependency on an expert to provide that correct answer or alternatively a judgment by the **Influencer** that if he or she hasn't been successful yet, it must be because of a poor strategy design or poor implementation skills. This thinking limits one's ability to notice other possibilities and all data, including data about the **Target**, the context, or the **Influencer's** goals. Third, many lawyers prefer to bring issues to closure quickly. This thinking limits Action Plan iterations and inhibits one from gathering and using critical data.

These default ways of thinking can create anxiety. Also, the tendency to fall back on these default ways of thinking increases as one feels more anxiety, which often happens when one feels the pressure of intense competition in the marketplace for jobs and clients. The only way to break the cycle is to think differently and notice when feelings of anxiety are present. When the feelings are present, employ a strategy for managing your emotions.

Although the idea of learning something new is appealing to most lawyers, many lawyers fight the idea of multiple iterations of a strategy. By nature and/or training lawyers are risk-adverse. The need for multiple iterations is interpreted as evidence of a mistake and needless risk-taking. In a lawyer's world, a mistake is malpractice and a measure of one's incompetence.

Intense competition can create anxiety, an unconscious blocker in one's decision-making process. In § 3:25 it was explained that when anxiety is present, a person will do anything to reduce it. A frequent response to anxiety is to pull up a highly emotionally charged memory of past ways of responding to anxiety, which for lawyers often means reverting to the idiosyncratic thinking that works so well when acting in one's professional capacity as a lawyer.

The lawyer mindset of believing in a single truth provable though the best advocacy actually creates a false choice between making a bad mistake and not collecting necessary data. Both doom a person to stagnation. Resolve the paradox by moderating each and experiment intelligently. You must embrace a willingness to take reasonable risks, which means you have to become smarter in evaluating the risks and benefits of any course of action.

The mindset of wanting to bring issues to closure quickly will also doom a perfectly good **Influence Strategy** to premature death. Instead of discarding a strategy, collect more data about what worked and what should be changed. Then try a new iteration as an experiment.

As you read the following case study, pay attention to examples of the role of Action Learning in collecting important data used to refine goals and develop action plans to reach those goals.

Case Study: Elizabeth Levy and Action Learning

Elizabeth Levy is Counsel at Siemens Health Care Diagnostics in Norwood, Massachusetts. She is responsible for providing advice on legal/business/compliance risks. She has learned through "trial and error" that she is "more influential when she doesn't try to tell others what they should do." A large part of designing an effective **Influence Strategy** hinges on your plan for collecting data about what your **Target** wants, needs, and expects, even in terms of being influenced. Liz learned to give an opinion and recommendation in a way that is suggestive instead of phrasing her advice in a demanding way or from a Formal Position or Expert **Power Base**. For example, she might say, "It seems to make sense if we do . . ." or "Given where we are, it suggests that . . . ." This is an example of one's use of Referent Power by carefully choosing the right language to express an idea so that the **Target** can hear the idea and decide to act in the desired way.

Liz learned to embrace trial and error through her experiences, which forced her to use trial and error. After attending an all-female liberal arts college and hating it, she took a summer job on a construction crew as a flag person and decided to study engineering as a result. After her sophomore year in college she transferred to a large state university and enrolled in engineering graduating with honors and a degree in mechanical engineering. Her parents were opposed to this transition and withdrew financial and emotional support. Relying only on her strength as a student and her ability to study anything and learn, she used a "bare knuckles/brute force approach" to adapt and succeed in unfamiliar environments. After working for eight years as an engineer, she was encouraged to consider law school by a patent attorney. Without the support of her parents, she learned to turn to others for the support she needed and, upon graduation from college, her employer paid for her law school tuition. She realized that the process that brought her success in college was not the process that worked in law school. She had "to try things" based on her own ideas and the advice that others gave her of what might work. Eventually she learned how to be successful in law school by using a process that made sense in that environment.

On graduation from law school, she took a job at a patent law firm and worked at two more firms over the next eight years, eventually making partner after five years. She then joined a very large international law firm as an Intellectual Property ("IP") partner and found it to be a virtual smorgasbord of interesting work experiences. She met her future husband at that firm and when they decided to marry, they knew they would both need a "wife" if they stayed at the firm, so she went in-house as senior patent counsel. After three years she moved from IP to the general/commercial legal side of the business and became a "mini GC" for that business.

Each transition allowed her to gather further data about her professional and personal goals. She tried one college and major and then another. She worked as an engineer and then attended law school. She worked in companies and law firms and figured out what worked in her personal life through trial and error and was eventually able to bring that lesson of how to learn to her professional life as an attorney, advising her clients.

Liz built on her strengths, in particular her ability to advance through hard work and her willingness to ask others for help. She used her personal strengths and her network **Power Base**. She also reflected on her actions and experiences to figure out what would work for her needs. Mistakes were inevitable, but not fatal. The "mistakes" and their consequences were data about what worked well and what did not. This data then informed future decisions.

The more data you collect about the wants, needs, and expectations of your **Targets** and yourself to incorporate into your **Influence Strategy** design, the more effective your plan will become in moving you closer to your goals. Collecting useful data is a result of keen observation, listening, and asking good questions. Collecting useful data and implementing the actions steps of an **Influence Strategy** in a way that is most effective is a result of having a good skill set. The Myers-Briggs Type Indicator ® and the Thomas-Kilmann Conflict Mode Instrument are excellent tools to improve the skills sets involved in collecting data and implementing action plans because they are helpful lenses for understanding human nature, yours and your **Target's**, better.

§ 5:3   The MBTI® lens

The MBTI® theory was referenced in §§ 2:9 and 4:6 as a useful assessment tool for developing self-awareness. This section explains the theory and instrument in greater detail. C.J. Jung, in 1923, published a book, Psychological Types, which looked at the differences in behavior preferences among people. Katherine Briggs and her daughter, Isabel Briggs Myers designed a psychological instrument, the Myers-Briggs Type Indicator (MBTI) ®, which measures these differences in scientifically rigorous and reliable terms. The instrument measures the way people interact with their internal and external worlds, perceive data from their worlds, and make decisions about the information they have gathered. The MBTI® theory and instrument are effective tools for **Influencers** to use to better understand the wants, needs, and expectations of **Targets**, better understand their interaction, perception, and decision-making preferences, and improve their strategic communication skills.

The MBTI® looks at communication processes through the lens of different preferences along four functional dichotomies.[1] There is an energy gathering function, a data collection function, a decision-making function, and a function for choosing between gathering data and making decisions. The best way to understand these preferences and to develop a modicum of self and other awareness of what the specific behaviors look and feel like is to participate in an MBTI® workshop, preferably one that focuses on strategic communication and that includes other lawyers. The first of the four functions is the energy gathering function of Extraversion and Introversion. People need energy to use in the perception and decision-making functions and the different preferences depend on whether the person gathers energy from her or his outer world (Extraversion) or the inner world of his or her mind (Introversion). Sensing and Intuition relate to the type of data a person prefers to gather from his or her world. Thinking and Feeling relate to the type of decision-making process a person prefers to use to makes sense of data and decide on actions. Judging and Perceiving relate to the preference a person has for making decisions or gathering data. Although there is not a true linearity to this communication process, we might say that without energy there would be no process at all. This begs the question of how and where people find the energy to gather data, make decisions about the data, and then act as a result of those decisions. They do it in two different ways, according to the MBTI® theory.

§ 5:4   The MBTI® lens—Extraversion and introversion: The energy gathering function

One might not think that whether someone gathers energy from his or her external world or internal world would have a significant effect on one's appearance and Referent **Power Base**,

---

[Section 5:3]

[1]There are four dichotomies, leading to Eight Type preferences in the MBTI®. The dichotomies are: Extravert vs. Introvert; Sensor vs. iNtuitive; Thinker vs. Feeler; and Judger vs. Perceiver. The bolded letter in each preference is what is used to report that preference in the instrument.

but it does. Many of the behaviors one associates with confidence come naturally to Extraverts. It is easy for an extravert to walk into a room and quickly speak up. Extraverts enjoy large gatherings of people and interacting with everyone in the room. Extraverts appear to have boundless energy when in public. Extraverts also tend to "think out loud." This means they may share their data gathering or decision-making process instead of quickly and directly answering a question, a characteristic often associated with decisiveness. Doing so may undermine an appearance of confidence.

Dean JoAnne Epps advises lawyers to determine the circumstances in which their natural instincts help or hurt and then make intentional adjustments. Introverts may tend to think before speaking and so appear to be slower to respond to questions, appearing less confident and decisive. They also may feel drained of their energy when in groups. Consequently, they can appear to be low-energy people.

On the positive side, Introverts may naturally appear to be excellent listeners. If asked a question, their measured response might be interpreted as thoughtful and with great depth. Extraverts may have a tendency to talk quickly and talk over others, not leaving enough space for others in the conversation to feel as though they were heard or important to the Extravert. Further, their quickness in responding to a serious question might lead the questioner to feel as if the answer received was not well thought out.

Differences Between Extraverts and Introverts

Extraverts	Introverts
Speak to think	Think then speak
Sociable	Boundaries
Interaction	Internally focused
Breadth	Depth
Multiple relationships	Limited relationships
Gregarious	Reflective
Appears to expend energy	Appears to conserve energy

§ 5:5 The MBTI® lens—Sensing and intuiting: The perceiving function

The essence of an **Influence Strategy** is to provide data for a **Target**. The intention of the **Influencer** is that the **Target** will react and respond to the data in a way that causes a particular decision to be made and a specific action to be taken. All people do not react to the same type of data in the same way. Different people have a preference for noticing and accepting one type of data over another.

Sensors prefer tangible data that relate to the five senses: sight, hearing, smell, touch, and taste. They are also present-reality and detail oriented, preferring to stay focused on what exists for them in their present place and time. Intuitives prefer data about the future possibilities, relationships, and concepts that a situation represents. They do not like getting bogged down in the details and would rather think about the big picture.

Everyone has a preference for one type of data or the other. Arguably, an **Influence Strategy** that is adjusted for the type of data that the **Target** will be looking for is more likely to be successful. This is the reason that speakers perceived as engaging often use both types of data. They may provide statistics and the concepts represented by those statistics. One needs a modicum of self-awareness to realize one's natural inclination and a modicum of self-regulation to provide what others might need.

Good decision-making is grounded in both types of data. Perhaps the biggest difference between Sensors and Intuitives is their orientation to time. A Sensor may think of time as an absolute, concrete, stand-alone moment. An Intuitive may think of time as a relationship between events. You might ask a Sensor and an Intuitive the time and end up with two very different answers. Both answers add value to any decision that depends on the time of an event. After all time is relative until you have an appointment to meet someone, who expects you to be present at an exact moment. The Sensor will look at his or her watch and may tell you the exact time of 1:07. The Intuitive may tell you that it's "a little past one." You can drop a $20 bill on the floor and ask a Sensor to describe it and you may get a detailed response that includes a list of everything from the several colors in the paper to the exact size, shape, and feel. An Intuitive's description might include something like, "it won't buy very much at the market." Both Sensors and Intuitives are capable of noticing body language and tone of voice. The difference is whether the person notices the sequential, realistic, and specific qualities or the random, conceptual, and general qualities of a person, place, or thing.

Differences Between Sensors and Intuitives

Sensors	Intuitives
Sequential	Random
Present	Future
Realistic	Conceptual
Perspiration	Inspiration
Actual	Theoretical
Down-to-earth	Head-in-clouds
Fact	Fantasy
Practicality	Ingenuity
Specific	General

§ 5:6   The MBTI® lens—Thinking and feeling: The decision-making function

The aim of an **Influence Strategy** is to affect the **Target's** decision-making process; therefore, knowing something about one's preferred way of decision-making and that of other people is important. According to the MBTI® there are two preferences for decision-making processes. Thinkers prefer to use a linear, logical, and analytical model for reaching decisions. Feelers, on the other hand, are guided toward a decision by their values. Thinkers feel and Feelers think. The nomenclature for the MBTI® decision-making function is unfortunate. There is no greater likelihood of reaching a good or bad decision using a model or values. Two people can reach the same decision, even if one is a Thinker and the other is a Feeler.

Feelers may try to avoid conflict and maintain harmony. Consequently, they naturally give weight to how a decision will affect people and relationships. At the extreme end, they may inadvertently slip into a Martyr thought pattern and elevate the other person's wants, needs, and expectations above their own. Thinkers are detached and often do not notice or may even embrace conflict as a model for discovering the objective truth. They may inadvertently slip into a Warrior state of mind and irreparably damage an important relationship with a decision and action. Many lawyers are Thinkers and this process is heavily embedded in the legal process. This dichotomy breaks down along gender lines, creating a risk that the implicit biases cause us to unconsciously expect women to behave as Feelers and men to behave as Thinkers. When they don't act consistently with our unconsciously held stereotypes, we unconsciously evaluate them negatively.

"At their best, the Thinking decision maker brings objectivity to any given decision-making situation and the Feeling decision maker brings an awareness of how that decision will be received by those whom it affects."[1] When the differences between any of the four dichotomies is expressed in a relationship, conflict arises; however, because there is a difference in the way that Thinkers and Feelers actually perceive and respond to conflict, the interaction can be incendiary. When you superimpose gender issues over this, you can see how a male Feeler and female Thinker can find themselves in a seemingly intractable dispute over what appears to others to be nothing at all. The following example is meant to be illustrative.

Callie and David are partners in a law firm. Callie has a strong preference for the Thinker end of the spectrum. David has a strong preference for the Feeler end of the spectrum. Callie and David are talking about the fact that they need to tell the remaining 40 partners the impact of the most recent financial data for the law firm.

David says, "This is important information. Every partner will want to hear it in person and will have questions about the impact on them."

Callie responds, "David, there isn't enough time in the day to speak to each partner individually about the financials. E-mail the information as soon as possible to everyone."

David, getting visibly agitated replies, " Callie, you just don't get it. Each partner needs to be reassured of his or her importance to the firm. They need to be told how they will be impacted by the change in cash flow."

Callie, now completed frustrated and feeling unheard says, "David, are you really going to spend an hour with every partner just to explain cash flow?" David thinks Callie is cold-hearted, and Callie thinks David is weak and worried about making everyone feel good.

At this point, Trudy says, "Stop the violent agreement! E-mail the financial data to the partners ahead of time and schedule some face-time for follow-up as needed." David and Callie smile and nod their heads, each thinking that Trudy has just agreed with their position.

[Section 5:6]

[1]Otto Kroeger and Janet M. Thuesen. Type Talk 32 (1988).

Differences Between Thinkers and Feelers

Thinkers	Feelers
Objective	Subjective
Firm-minded	Fair-hearted
Laws	Circumstances
Firmness	Persuasion
Just	Humane
Clarity	Harmony
Critique	Appreciative
Policy	Social Values
Detached	Involved

§ 5:7   The MBTI® lens—Thinking and feeling: The decision-making function—Judging and perceiving: The preference to make decisions or gather data

The best **Influence Strategy** will fail if the **Influencer** inadvertently undermines his or her Referent Power. One's preference for gathering data rather than making decisions might have this effect among a group of lawyers. Judgers are people who prefer to make decisions and Perceivers are people who prefer to gather data. More lawyers are Judgers than are Perceivers. This is the function that "you most naturally use as you relate to the outer world, verbally and behaviorally." Its use creates "the most significant source of interpersonal tension" and is most obvious to other people.[1] Since more lawyers are Judgers and Judgers prefer to make decisions quickly, this behavior— because it is in the majority among lawyers—becomes positively adjudged as sign of decisiveness and competence. People often think that their behavior is the ideal behavior. When the behavior is exhibited by a majority of people in a group, it is not surprising for it to be prescribed behavior. A Perceiver who is also an Extravert is likely to share his or her process of responding to a question with a search for more data. There is a difference between being able to make a decision and preferring to collect more data rather than make a decision, but that goes unnoticed and one's Referent Power is inadvertently undermined.

If you have created a structured, ordered, scheduled, controlled, and planned world for yourself and if you are decisive, deliberate,

---

[Section 5:7]

[1]Otto Kroeger & Janet M. Thuesen. Type Talk 40 (1988).

and able to make decisions with little stress, then chances are that you are a Judger. It is likely that you plan your work, organize your playtime, and believe that there is a right and wrong process, procedure, and schedule for everything. You work then you play.

On the other hand, if you prefer being flexible, spontaneous, and adapting to the situation of the moment rather than making and sticking to a particular plan, you are probably a Perceiver. It is likely that you prefer to wait and see what needs to be done, collect more information about how to solve a particular problem, and allow the right possibilities to emerge when the last possible moment to make a decision arrives. You can turn your work into play.

Targets who have a preference for Judging may be more susceptible to influence in the nature of decisive behavior while Perceivers may be looking for more data. It's important to listen carefully and determine what someone wants, needs, and expects in aid of reaching the decision that is the aim of an **Influence Strategy**. If you notice a Judging preference, try to determine whether the person has a Thinking or Feeling preference. If your **Target** has a Thinking preference, conflict in the nature of taking the role of Devil's advocate may be effective for testing assumptions and offering alternatives. If your **Target** has a Feeling preference, it is likely that he or she will want to avoid conflict and maintain harmony in relationships. Showing the **Target** how the decisions you want her or him to make will avoid conflict and maintain harmonious relationships may be effective.

Targets who have a preference for Perceiving may be less interested in reaching any decision. One's **Influence Strategy** ought to include nudging the person closer to a decision. Sensors will want statistics, diagrams, drawings, and photographs. Intuitives will want to talk about future possibilities, concepts, and the relationships among ideas.

Differences Between Judges and Perceivers

Judgers	Perceivers
Resolved	Pending
Decided	Wait and see
Control	Adapt
Closure	Possibilities
Planned	Open-ended
Structure	Go with flow

Judgers	Perceivers
Definite	Tentative
Scheduled	Spontaneous
Deadline.	Deadline?
Fixed	Flexible

Worksheet: Influence Strategies for Decision-Making and Data Collection Preferences in Targets

1. Is your **Target** a Judger or Perceiver? Why?

   a. Does **Target** appear to be deadline-focused and structured? Does he or she try to bring issues to closure? Is he or she someone who plans ahead, uses checklists, and schedules time clearly and rigidly? If so, he or she is more likely a Judger.

   b. Does **Target** appear to adapt to situations in the moment, focus on the here and now, and go with the flow? Does he or she try to avoid making decisions? Is he or she spontaneous and flexible? If so, he or she is more likely a Perceiver.

2. If a Judger, is your **Target** a Thinker or Feeler? Why?

   a. Does **Target** express objectivity as a cherished value? Does he or she appear to use analytical models like general policies, laws, rules, or guidelines to weigh evidence and reach a conclusion? Does he or she seek clarity? If so, your **Target** is likely a Thinker.

   b. Does your **Target** express harmony and compassion for others as a driving value? Does he or she avoid conflict? Does he or she like to consider the special circumstances of the people who will be affected by the decision? If so, your **Target** is likely a Feeler.

3. If your **Target** is Judger, which actions should you consider adding to your strategic influence plan to help meet that person's wants, needs, and expectations of moving to a decision and closure quickly?

4. If your **Target** is a Judger, which actions should you consider adding to your strategic influence plan to address the possibility that your **Target** will move to closure and the wrong decision too quickly and miss critical data?

5. If your **Target** is a Thinker, what models is he or she using? What questions will you ask to figure out which models are being used? What will you listen or look for to give you clues about which models are being used? Will you offer different models that might result in a decision more favor-

able to you? Why or why not? How will you present the idea of using a different model?

6. If your **Target** is a Thinker, which logical arguments will you offer to plug into your **Target's** models?

7. If your **Target** is a Thinker, should you play Devil's advocate to create conflict? Why or why not? How will you do it to move your **Target** closer to the decision you want, i.e., will challenging his or her flawed models or analysis move him or her closer to the decision and outcome you want? Is there a way to get your **Target** to challenge his or her models himself or herself? How?

8. If your **Target** is a Feeler, which values is he or she using to drive the decision making process? What questions will you ask to figure out which values are being used? What will you listen or look for to give you clues about which values are being used? Will you offer different values that might result in a decision more favorable to you? Why or why not? How will you present the idea of using different values, especially given the likely value of maintaining harmony and avoiding conflict?

9. If your **Target** is a Feeler, how will you communicate in a way that maintains harmony and avoids conflict? How will you communicate that you value the relationship with your **Target**?

10. If a Perceiver, is your **Target** a Sensor or an Intuitive? Why?

   a. Does your **Target** talk about the specific characteristics of what he or she sees, hears, feels, tastes, and smells in the moment and situation being described? Does he or she talk about time in exact terms? If so, your **Target** is likely a Sensor.

   b. Does your **Target** talk about the general ideas, themes, concepts, and future possibilities when describing any situation? Does he or she talk about time in relative terms? If so, your **Target** is likely an Intuitive.

11. If your **Target** is a Perceiver, which actions should you consider adding to your strategic influence plan to help meet that person's wants, needs, and expectations to collect more data?

12. If your **Target** is a Perceiver, which actions should you consider adding to your strategic influence plan to address your **Target's** possible avoidance of making any decision?

13. If your **Target** is a Sensor, which type of data does he or she want, need, or expect? What questions will you ask to

figure out which data he or she wants, needs, or expects?
What will you listen or look for to give you clues about
which data are being sought? Will you offer additional data
that might results in a decision more favorable to you?
Why or why not?

14. If your **Target** is a Sensor, which type of data will you use
and how will you present additional data? Does your **Target** have a preference for visual or heard data? If so, which
type (words, photographs, diagrams, pictures)? It is usually
best to present the data in an orderly fashion to a Sensor.

15. If your **Target** is an Intuitive, what questions will you ask
to figure out what your **Target** wants, need, or expects?
What themes are emerging from what your **Target** is telling or asking you? What are the connections and patterns
that your **Target** appears to be noticing? Brainstorming
may be welcome to an Intuitive. What will you do to help
your **Target** to "brainstorm" the ideas that will help you?

§ 5:8   The Thomas-Kilmann Conflict Mode lens

Influence Strategies are only necessary when a **Target** and
Influencer have different concerns or desires.[1] The difference
may be present because the **Target** has not been informed of the
Influencer's wants, needs, or expectations or because the **Target**
and the **Influencer** want, need, and expect different things.
When a difference in thinking is present, an effective **Influence
Strategy** includes a set of action steps to address the respective
conflict responses that may arise. The Thomas-Kilmann Conflict
Mode Instrument ("TKI") was first mentioned in § 2:9 as a useful
self-assessment tool for understanding one's preferences for noticing and responding to conflict. This section will explain the tool
in greater detail. The TKI explains the different behavior preferences that people have toward conflict. It describes the different
behaviors according to the relative amounts of "assertiveness, the
extent to which the individual attempts to satisfy his or her own
concerns, and cooperativeness, the extent to which the individual
attempts to satisfy the other person's concerns."[2] The instrument,
according to the theory, categorizes behaviors into five different
ways of handling conflict: (1) Competing; (2) Compromising; (3)
Collaborating; (4) Avoiding; and (5) Accommodating.

[Section 5:8]

[1]Thomas-Killman Conflict Workshop Facilitator's Guide RM-2.

[2]Marvin D. Dunnette. The Handbook of Industrial and Organizational
Psychology (1976).

We expect to face conflict in the courtroom or when we're negotiating a transaction with our opposing counsel. In situations that arise out of our professional role as a lawyer, we have been taught how to respond to it. In particular, we have been taught in law school to respond to conflict with a competing or a compromising orientation. There are three other options. Negotiations are often more fruitful with a collaborating orientation. Each option has its place and time. Having an awareness of your own default mode of responding to conflict, being able to judge which conflict mode someone else is using, being able to use all five responses effectively, and knowing which response to use based upon an analysis of the situation is a required skill set for anyone expecting to be an effective **Influencer**. The rest of this section explains the distinguishing features of the five conflict modes.

Competing behavior is assertive and uncooperative. It appears as though the individual is compelled to win his or her position. Signs of a competing orientation are arguing or debate, asserting one's opinions or feelings, appearing intractable, and acting with quick decision and action. It is an appropriate choice when one's intention is to emphasize or use one's Formal Position or Expert Power. Its decisive nature makes it useful in times where immediate action is critical. An **Influencer** or a **Target** may be motivated to use a Competing stance to win a position, appear as an expert, or emphasize one's hierarchical position. Alternatively, it may be a sign of anxiety. As explained in § 3:25, anxiety produces unconscious blockers. Those blockers are automatic responses to a situation, which may be the competing or Warrior archetype behavior lawyers are taught to use to address conflict. Negative consequences of this orientation are a limitation on valuable feedback from others, reduced ability to learn from mistakes and improve performance, and the triggering of back channel influencing strategies.

Compromising behavior is a combination of assertive and cooperative. The conflict is resolved with a solution that is expedient, mutually acceptable, and partially satisfies both parties. It looks like an attempt to find a middle ground, assess a value, and make concessions. It avoids confrontations and at times misses the complete picture, diminishes trust, and creates a cynical climate. It's an appropriate choice when time is of the essence, the risks of confrontation outweigh the benefits, there is no need for additional data about the wants, needs, and expectations of the people involved, and trust building is not a goal. It takes a significant amount of time and mutual listening, asking question about wants, needs, expectations, and ideas to develop trust in any relationship.

Collaborating is a combination of assertive and cooperative behaviors. It appears as an attempt by an **Influencer** to work with the **Target** to find a solution that fully satisfies the interests of both. It's an **Influence Strategy** that is designed to strengthen relationships, gain commitment to a particular decision by merging perspectives, develop mutual learning, and integrate solutions. It is a time-consuming process. Communication includes alternatively sharing interests and inquiring into the interests of the **Target**. It appears as listening, understanding, and empathizing and a search for the deeper motivations, concerns, and interests. Collaborating behavior may be motivated by a desire to deepen a relationship, learn from each other's insights or find a creative solution. Collaborating behavior may be motivated by a belief that consensus decisions are better, a desire to share data, beliefs that people are allies or potential allies, or a desire to gather data rather than to make an immediate decision. It is an effective use of one's MBTI® Perceiving function, despite a pending question in contrast to creating an appearance of incompetence or indecisiveness.

Avoiding is unassertive and uncooperative. The behavior either does not address or denies the conflict. It may also diplomatically sidestep or postpone dealing with an issue until the timing is better. The behavior is the absence of requests, demands, argument, or questions. It may appear as cautious behavior or as saving time for more important issues. It reduces tensions rather than escalating them. Avoiding an issue leaves it unresolved. Avoiding may be difficult for someone who prefers to make decisions and bring issues to closure quickly, the preference of an MBTI® Judger or for someone who finds clarity and understanding through conflict and debate, like a Thinker. A Feeler may use avoiding behavior to preserve harmony.

Accommodating behavior is unassertive and cooperative; it is the polar opposite of Competing. It appears as if the person is ignoring his or her own concerns to satisfy the concerns of the other person. It may look like the Martyr archetype or the Feeler's attempt to preserve harmony and relationships. Examples of the behavior are selfless generosity, complying with the other's demands, or yielding to another's point of view. It may convey reasonableness, fear, weakness, or goodwill. It is a transfer of power, which might be a wise strategy especially if the issue is relatively unimportant to the **Influencer.**

Ideally, one will learn enough self-awareness and control to choose the best conflict strategy for each conflict situation. This is an especially important skill for anyone who works in government or a large organization.

Case Study: Laura—Influence and a Creative Spark

Laura is the division counsel to a health care company and a member of the executive leadership team that sets strategy for the business. She is expected to help her business find creative ways to address conflict so that it can reach its overall strategic goals. As a lawyer, she participates on a lot of negotiating teams because of her legal expertise but is expected to bring much more value than that to the table. She creates value by looking beyond articulated positions of the other party and trying to understand what the party really needs and what the party can offer to create a mutually beneficial agreement.

Developing a deep understanding of another party depends on collecting sufficient data "through homework, historical knowledge, and what is said at the table." It is also a result of paying attention to body language, emotions, and her gut intuition. Laura pays attention to nonverbal cues, such as whether someone's arms are crossed, if the person makes eye contact, where the person is focusing attention, how directly or indirectly a person answers questions, and how people interact with others in the room.

Using that data to achieve the outcome that her client needs or wants may mean inspiring the other party to change his or her mind on issues of importance to Laura's clients, while preserving what that party needs to structure an agreement. For example, her organization needed to reach an agreement with a supplier for a particular product at a certain price. Through homework and conversations, it was clear that the supplier had a limited ability to adjust the product's price as much as Laura's organization needed. However, through homework, historical knowledge, and listening at the table, data emerged that the supplier had marketing dollars available for the deal. They were able to structure an agreement that was mutually beneficial by using the marketing dollars instead of adjusting the price of the product.

Questions

1. What was the conflict situation?
2. What approaches were used to address the conflict?

Worksheet: Conflict and Influence Strategies

1. Think of a current situation that you characterize as a conflict situation. Describe it. Are there other ways to think about the situation?
2. Which of the five conflict behaviors do you notice in others?

Who is using the behavior? What are the signs? What are the possible reasons?

3. Which of the five conflict behaviors do you notice in yourself? What are the signs? What are the reasons?
4. Which of the five conflict behaviors aren't you using? Why?
5. Is there a different behavior that you think might be more effective? What? Why would it work? Why would the **Target** respond more favorably to it?

Use the table below to help you analyze conflict situations.

Behavior	Signs	Will Target respond favorably to behavior?	Possible Reasons for Target's response
Competing			
Compromising			
Collaborating			
Avoiding			
Accommodating			

§ 5:9 Strategic communication and Influence Strategies

Influence Strategies depend on having a solid skill set in strategic communication. The self-awareness gained by attending workshops that use the MBTI® and TKI is part of developing strategic communication skills. As a process, there are two parts to strategic communication: effective listening and giving feedback effectively.

§ 5:10 Strategic communication and Influence Strategies—Effective listening: Discovering information about a Target's wants, needs, and expectations

Collecting data and making sense of it is a critical component of any **Influence Strategy**. It is difficult, if not impossible, to effectively influence anyone without a clear understanding of what he or she needs, wants, expects, thinks, and feels. This is true for everything from effective cross selling to meeting expectations for a stellar job performance evaluation. As lawyers, we have developed a type of listening skill that is an extremely effective tool for supporting our goal of effectively advocating a particular position. This type of listening is targeted listening. It is constantly judging the speaker's words against a legal or other model of what is right and directing the conversation to follow a particular path.

Targeted listening is in sharp contrast to the type of listening skill that is valuable for collecting data about the wants, needs, and expectations of a person, regardless of whether that person is empowered to drive business opportunities in your direction, hire you into a particular position, give you a bonus, put you on an important project, give you opportunities to lead, evaluate you favorably, or advance your career with a formal promotion. Effective listening skills outside of the courtroom are invaluable when you want to moderate the level of conflict, make someone feel important, and be perceived as likeable. This second type of listening skill is empathic listening. Carl Rogers, a psychologist, recognized its value and created a model for developing the skill. Empathy is a two-part skill. First, it is the capacity, figuratively speaking, to stand in the shoes of another whose life experiences have been very different. Second, it is the ability to understand that person's view without any judgment.

Empathic listening is a foundational skill in every leadership responsibility from creating and getting buy-in for a strategic vision to implementing a plan for business development. The process for empathic listening is a three-step process: (1) attentive listening, (2) asking effective diagnostic questions, and (3) offering a solution. Lawyers, as a group, tend to skip the first two steps, jump to the third, and then advocate for why their solution is the right one.

One of the hardest skills for a lawyer is to be able to stay in the attentive listening phase for a sufficient amount of time. We have a tendency to shift inadvertently to targeted listening and offer a solution or sympathy, share a story of how we faced a similar challenge, or sit quietly so that the other person will quickly finish talking. Each reflects impatience, which appears in body language. The tendency becomes even stronger when we are worried about time. Listening takes time and time is money for lawyers.

The key to listening is to allow people to think through their problems openly and allow them to try to solve them on their own, while acknowledging their feelings. Empathic listening motivates the speaker to share his or her experience, wants, needs, and expectations without feeling judged, interrupted, or as if the conversation is being directed by the listener. This important data is what builds deep relationships with clients, referral sources, and colleagues.

As lawyers, we assume that because we are experienced negotiators, drafters of interrogatories, deposition-takers, and direct and cross-examiners in a courtroom, we are excellent data collectors and diagnosticians in all interpersonal relationships. Our keenly developed targeted listening skill makes us less effective. Effective diagnostic actions include questions, comments, and body language. Effective questions are open-ended, analytical, and invitations for the person to say more. Effective comments are those that show empathy and understanding. Effective body language shows interest in the other person.

The underlying theme is that good listeners are inquisitive listeners, who assume that they need more information from the speaker before they can truly understand the meaning of an action, event, or word in the same way that the speaker does. Examples of good investigative questions ask what the speaker would like to do, what outcome he or she would like, what efforts have been made to get that outcome, what is really bothering the speaker, how he or she is feeling, what else the speaker can say about the situation, and what options the speaker sees. Good comments summarize the speaker's words and feelings and show an understanding that those feelings are possible. Effective body language includes genuine warmth, a smile and softer voice, leaning toward the speaker, and physical touch, if appropriate. Ineffective body language conveys boredom, distraction, and judgment.

There are additional techniques that will help the speaker share more with you. These include the use of dangling questions that allow the listener to finish a sentence. Another technique is to directly ask the person to tell you more or acknowledge that what he or she has said is interesting to you. Yet, another effective technique is to repeat a phrase or key word used by the speaker. Finally, respecting the speaker's pauses, without jumping in to eliminate the silence, is a very helpful signal of interest in the speaker's situation.

Perhaps the most difficult skill for a lawyer is learning why and how to suspend judgment. This is the opposite of what we do as lawyers. We generally are paid to take a side and argue a position. Also, we generally feel frustrated when the speaker seems blind to our perceptions of common sense.

The reason to suspend judgment is that the outcome usually is more beneficial in the long run. People need to feel heard and prefer to feel like they participated in solving their own problems. Indeed, this is how people learn. Once you have truly listened, you can always share your concerns from your perspective. Suspending judgment is a skill that can be developed through workshops, coaching, and practice. Effective listening is the first part to relationship-building communication. The second part is learning how to give feedback effectively.

§ 5:11 Strategic communication and Influence Strategies—Giving feedback effectively

Feedback is data. Building relationships requires sharing data about the respective wants, needs, expectations, and thinking of the parties involved. As lawyers, we are often asked for feedback in the nature of deconstructing our own and others' arguments. This type of feedback does not deepen relationships and may even harm them. When the goal of feedback is to influence a person, behavioral feedback is more effective. The goal is to change the **Target's** behavior, not to test the strength of the **Target's** position.

There are three parts to giving effective feedback: (1) stating your observation; (2) explaining the effect it has on you; and (3) identifying and asking for different behavior in the future. Each part requires clarity and specificity in communication.

Stick to the facts when stating your observation and then do so with clarity and specificity. Describe the behavior of the **Target** with an example and without sharing your conclusions or judgments about the behavior. Use "I" statements. Share only one observation at a time. Do not provide too much data and overwhelm the listener with what will likely be perceived as unfair criticism. For example, if you were not chosen to lead a "make your career project," you might say to the decision maker, "I noticed that you didn't choose me to be on the SuperCo deal team."

Next, explain the effect that the other person's behavior has on you. Doing this means that you acknowledge your part in the perception rather than laying blame on the other person. It also means avoiding judgment and finding fault. When you offer feedback that openly acknowledges that the observation and reaction is about you, you are implicitly acknowledging the fact that others may perceive and respond differently than you did. Explain your beliefs, biases, lenses, and hidden assumptions without assuming that your beliefs are right and the other person's are wrong. This allows the receiver to draw his or her own conclusions and decide whether or not he or she is motivated to change his or her behavior. To continue with the prior example, you might say, "I noticed that you didn't choose me to be on the SuperCo deal team. I recall your telling me that if I proved myself on the LittleCo matter, that you would put me on the next SuperCo deal. I believe that I proved myself on LittleCo by doing (fill in the blank). I was surprised and disappointed that you seemed to choose not to put me on the SuperCo team today."

Finally, ask for what you want. Nobody ever figured out what to do on the basis of being told what not to do. Nobody will know what you want until you tell them. This is the classic mistake of performance evaluations and relationships that break with the weight of too much interpersonal criticism. The goal of feedback is to get the other person to behave differently in the future. Choose behavior that the person has the power to change, rather than raising issues outside of the person's control. Be clear and specific about the behavior you would like to see in the future and how it will be helpful to you and/or the other person. What exactly would you like the person to do differently in the future? To finish the example, you might say, "I noticed that you didn't choose me to be on the SuperCo deal team. I recall your telling me that if I proved myself on the LittleCo matter, that you would put me on the next SuperCo deal. I believe that I proved myself on LittleCo by doing (fill in the blank). I was surprised and disappointed that you seemed to choose not to put me on the SuperCo team today. I would like to know why I wasn't chosen for the team and what you need to see from me to put me on the next SuperCo matter."

To help you give more effective feedback to others, here is a list of Dos and Don'ts.

Feedback Dos and Don'ts

DO	DON'T
Be specific in describing the behavior you would like to see change; provide examples.	Give general or vague feedback.
Keep it short, one item at a time.	Provide too much data.
Keep it present, about the here and now.	Do not dredge up the past.
Own your part in the perception.	Lay blame on the other person.
Avoid judgment.	Find fault.
Choose behavior that the person has power to change.	Raise issues outside of the person's control.
Explain your lenses, biases, and underlying assumptions.	Assume that your beliefs are right and the other person's beliefs are wrong.
Assume good motives in others. We all do our best.	Attribute negative intentions to other person.

§ 5:12 Specific Influence Strategies for lawyers

Lawyers in law firms might be interested in knowing how to advance their careers regardless of whether that means getting from associate to partner, adjunct to tenured professor, or into a leadership role as head of a department or organization. They might also be interested in developing a book of business or otherwise effectively marketing themselves for a particular job. This section looks at few specific **Influence Strategies**. Don't forget that the effective implementation of all effective strategies is an Action Learning process of intelligent experimentation.

§ 5:13 Specific Influence Strategies for lawyers— Advancing your career

Advancing your career begins with giving yourself permission to be ambitious and setting goals as Dean of Temple Law School, JoAnne Epps, advises students. "Dream about what kind of life you would like to have and think about the best way to achieve it." It is the difference between searching for and creating your opportunities and being completely reactive to the opportunities that may or may not fall into your lap. It may be difficult to think clearly of the future, especially without role models and mentors, which tend to be more available to those people with more privileges in terms of social identity and economics. Dean Epps advises students to think about the characteristics of your life that will make you happy. She suggests asking these questions. Do you want to be "furiously busy doing great and important things?" Is it important to you to have a job that allows you "to have broad impact or will you be happy helping one person solve a problem?" Is it important for you to have intellectually challenging work? If so, do you realize that this may be a lonely life? Do you crave social interaction? It is easier to seek out, find, and seize opportunities if you have an idea of the life that you would like to create. Self-awareness takes self-reflection after having experiences. This means that it is important for you to create the conditions so that you are able to have new and varied experiences.

Once you have an idea of your vision of the kind of life that will bring you happiness, you will need to gather information about the opportunities, power, and responsibilities that attach to any specific job position under consideration and consider whether they will bring you the kind of life that you want. Where will you look for this information? Who will you ask? Every career level has certain performance expectations. These may include billable hours (in a law firm), face-time in the organization, having had particular work experiences, publishing, public appearances, bringing in business to the organization, managing a budget well, managing teams, face time with clients of the organization, relationships, and outside activities. You must design a plan to gather the pertinent data.

Next, you will need to consider the prerequisites, in addition to having a required level of expertise and competence for the position. Consider those prerequisites in terms of developing and expanding your **Power Bases**. Laura wanted to move in-house after four years of law firm experience managing all phases and types of large commercial litigation matters, dealing extensively with in-house legal departments and business people, and making strategy decisions based on the analysis of complex factual and legal issues. Specifically, she wanted a position that involved counseling and advising a business, in addition to litigation management. She thought that she had the right skill set and résumé and if only the recruiters would put her forward for the right jobs, she would be able to convince anyone that she was the right candidate for the job. But somehow the interviews never came through. Laura eventually landed an in-house position after a few more years, because she had met and interacted with a manager at the organization in a strategy meeting for the multiple defendants involved in litigation together. Her Network Position power was a critical prerequisite to attaining her goal.

Once you have identified a specific position or type of position that you want to attain, where is it and what are the prerequisites? Where is this information located? Who will you ask? Do you need to consider moving outside of your current organization; perhaps a lateral move is necessary? Do you need additional experience or to expand your networks?

What decisions must be made in your favor and by whom before you will be able to satisfy critical performance expectations for a promotion? Who has the decision-making power? How will those decisions be made? How will he, she, or they be susceptible to your influence? Which of your **Power Bases** should you use in what particular **Influence Strategy** for each person that matters? Do you first need to develop additional skills of a substantive nature or to support your influence process? Which skills do you need to develop? What is your action plan for developing those skills? Do you need a mentor or sponsor? What is your action plan for getting the right person or persons to mentor or sponsor you? These are examples of some of the questions that you will need to answer to advance your career.

§ 5:14 Specific Influence Strategies for lawyers— Developing business or marketing yourself effectively

Developing business is really about marketing yourself and your law firm, which for business development purposes is an extension of you, effectively. The first step is being clear about your identity: who you are, what you do, and how you do it that is different and better from everyone else. The second step is being able to communicate your identity clearly and influentially and in a way that lands favorably on each **Target**. The third step is to build deep and mutually beneficial relationships with your **Targets**. This is part of developing your Network Position power explained earlier in the book.

Worksheet: Developing Your Identity Story

1. Answer the following questions.

Who am I? What are my values? What matters to me most?

_____

_____

_____

What do I do? How do I do it? How do I do it differently and better than anyone else?

_____

_____

_____

What do I want in general? What do I want specifically from a particular **Target**?

_____

_____

_____

How can I be helpful to others generally? How can I be helpful to a particular **Target**?

_____

_____

_____

2. Using the answers to the questions, write a 30-second answer to any question about who you are or what you do that a stranger might ask you.
3. With a particular **Target** in mind, develop an action plan to market yourself to that person. Do you need to gather data about the **Target**? What do you want to learn and how will you gather the information? What does your **Target** want, need, and expect? What does your **Target** want to know about you and your organization? Do you need to gather data from your colleagues to be able to effectively cross-sell your organization as part of the process of marketing yourself?

Worksheet: Cross-Selling Your Firm

Answer the following questions. For each question: What is your action plan for gathering the data to be able to answer this question? Where will you look for the data? Who will you speak to? What questions will you ask?

1. What stands out about the firm's values and culture?

_____

_____

2. What does the firm do? How does the firm do it? How does the firm do it differently and better than any other firm? Who are the clients? Why is the firm the "best fit" for its clients?

_____

_____

3. What does the practice group do? How does the practice group do it? How does the group do it differently and better than the

same practice groups in other firms? Who are the clients? Why is the practice group the "best fit" for its clients?

_____

_____

_____

4. What does this lawyer do? How does she or he do it? How does he or she do it differently and better than other lawyers in other firms? Who are her or his clients? Why is this lawyer the "best fit" for his or her clients?

_____

_____

_____

5. Who is an ideal client for the firm? The practice group? This lawyer? Why?

_____

_____

_____

6. Where should I go to meet ideal clients or referral sources of ideal clients?

_____

_____

_____

7. Using the answers to the questions, write a 30-second answer to any question about the firm, a practice group, or a lawyer that an ideal client or referral source might ask you.
8. If you have a particular **Target** in mind, develop an action plan to market your firm, practice group, or a lawyer to that person. Do you need to gather data about the **Target**? What do you want to learn and how will you gather the information? What does your **Target** want, need, and expect? What will your **Target** want to know about the firm, the practice, the lawyer, and you? Do you need to gather data from your colleagues to be able to effectively cross-sell your organization?

§ 5:15 Specific Influence Strategies for lawyers— Developing sponsor relationships

Not everyone falls into relationships with sponsors. Sponsors, also called champions, can make a significant difference in someone's career success, as described in some of the stories in this book. There are steps to take to develop sponsorship relationships and having such a strategy can only help.

Laura noticed that throughout her career there were people who believed in her and gave her opportunities that others were not given. She notes "someone has to believe in your full set of skills before they will champion you and you need to solicit feedback to learn where they see your strengths and invite constructive feedback on where you can improve." When they notice that you are taking their advice and working hard to improve, you may be able to convert them into a champion. Laura thinks that it is important to notice with whom you are interacting regularly and pay attention to how they interact with you. Are they pushing you and giving you extra growth opportunities? Are you showing them appreciation for doing so? When you notice this happening, it is time to ask for feedback. As they feel more appreciated, they will become more invested in you and your success. As this happens, the dialogue expands into a two-way street and moves past mentorship into sponsorship.

Gary Levin would agree and suggests that sponsorship starts with working with someone who starts to believe in your work. He suggests keeping your eyes open for the right person to work with and then express an interest in working with him or her. Keep your eyes open. You can tell where the power is in a law firm.

Worksheet: Developing the Sponsor Relationship

Answer the following questions to help you locate people who would be good sponsors and develop relationships with them.

1. Who are the powerful people within your organization?
2. Who are the people whose work is interesting to you? This could be legal work or leadership work.
3. Who are the people that are showing an interest in you and your career?

The overlap between the people identified in response to question #1 and those identified in response to #2 are good potential sponsors for you.

4. Identify the opportunities to work with any of your potential sponsors. Where are they? What are they?
5. Even if you are not able to identify any opportunities to work with your potential sponsor, are there any opportunities to ask him or her for advice? Is it possible to try to develop a mentoring relationship with the person? What could you do to try to develop a mentoring relationship with the person?
6. If you receive advice, what will you do to show the person that you are taking the advice and how it has been effective for you? What will you do to show your appreciation to the person?

7. As you work with your potential sponsor, identify the opportunities to ask for feedback on your performance, both as a lawyer and as a leader. If and when you receive feedback, be prepared to accept and show your appreciations, regardless of the content.

8. What will you do to show an interest in your potential sponsor as a person? What will you do to make the relationship mutually beneficial?

§ 5:16 Specific Influence Strategies for lawyers— Tracking your success

Tracking your successes is an important step of an action learning process because it is a way to capture information about the thinking and actions that worked for you in a particular situation. It is also important to capture data that you will need for your **Influence Strategy** to positively affect your performance evaluations. Preparing a written list of your accomplishments with details is a way to remember them, because people tend to forget tasks that are completed. The Zeigarnik effect is the phenomenon of remembering incomplete tasks and forgetting the completed ones.[1] Jane Dalton suggests that every lawyer keep a list of every accomplishment. "I often assumed when I did a good job, that it would be remembered, which of course, is not always the case. In fact, I often forgot my accomplishments because they were completed." Be your best advocate, ask for what you want, set goals, and go after them. Jane says, "if you do not set the direction you want to go, others will set it for you and they do not necessarily have your best interests in mind." I couldn't agree more.

§ 5:17 Conclusion

Using power and influence effectively is a process built on a set of skills and a way of thinking. Anyone can learn the skills and, through practice, become more proficient with the influence process. Learning anything is mostly about being willing to take risks and intelligently experiment until you are doing what you want to do the way that you want to do it; whether that means landing a dream client or job or just living your life in a way that brings you happiness.

[Section 5:16]

[1]Bluma V. Zeigarnik. Über das Behalten von erledigten und unerledigten Handlungen (The Retention of Completed and Uncompleted Activities). 9 Psychologische Forschung 1-85 (1927).

Index